The Barry Story

By
Martin Beckett

Published 2010   ISBN 978-0-946184-42-2

Published by
Kingfisher Productions

Watershed Mill, Settle, North Yorkshire BD24 9LR
www.railwayvideo.com

INTRODUCTION

The fascination which Barry and its steam locomotives has held for railway enthusiasts in recent years needs no emphasising by us. The first edition of this book was published in 1982 in a much smaller paperback. This edition is published some 30 years later and includes the tenth edition of The Barry List, so the complete story is now available for the first time in one publication. There are no more locomotives waiting for rescue in the yards with all 213 now in private hands, following the final departure of ex-GWR small prairie tank No. 5553 in January 1990 - a remarkable achievement. Without doubt, it has been a tremendous stimulus to the railway preservation movement and will ensure future development. Our purpose in writing this book has been to trace the historical background to the dock and railway systems of Barry, and to outline how they came to be used for the disposal of redundant steam locomotives. In presenting the book to its readers we hope that some of the interesting personalities and events which make up the railway history of Barry will be brought to the knowledge of a wider circle of railway enthusiasts. We hope also that it will be found informative on what is, after all, a unique phenomenon in recent railway history.

Many friends and correspondents have supplied valuable information about Barry over the years, too numerous to mention here. Dozens of enthusiasts wrote in to us from the early 1970s with their observations and sometimes photographs which helped the compilation of not only *The Barry Story*, but ten editions of *The Barry List*. We are also grateful to the Public Records Office, Kew, and to the Reference Libraries at Barry and Cardiff for research facilities.

We must, finally, thank the Woodham family for their help in recent years. Neta, Dai's wife, kindly loaned the family archive of photographs, some of which appear in this book and which give a great insight into the earlier years of Woodham Brothers.

Martin Beckett and Roger Hardingham
August 2010

Above: The town of Barry forms a backdrop to an early scene of Woodham's breaking up wagons on one of the old tip lines in the late 1950s.

Frontispiece: A proud Dai Woodham on site at Barry, 1950s.   *Woodham family collection*

Chapter One
BARRY IN HISTORY

The derivation of the name of the town has been attributed, according to the second edition (1838) of Carlisle's Topographical Dictionary of Wales, to *St. Baruch*, a holy hermit who lived in the area around 700 A.D. In mediaeval times the land was in the possession of the de Barri family, one of whose most notable members was the monk Giraldus Cambrensis who travelled widely in Wales during the twelfth century. Giraldus, or Gerald the Welshman as he is perhaps better known, described Barry Island as follows:

"On Barry Island there is a narrow chink or cleft, to which if you place your ear you will perceive the noise of smiths at work. Sometimes the blowing of bellows, sometimes the stroke of hammers, and fires fiercely burning in furnaces; sometimes the most harmonious sounds, like those of various instruments of music."

He goes on to say that these sounds were made by the fairies or mountain spirits engaged on building the brazen wall intended by the prophet Merlin for the perpetual defence of Britain. Fanciful these theories may be, but parts of Gerald's description could well be applied to certain activities of recent times which have brought the name of Barry to the attention of every railway enthusiast in the country!

Steam and sail in No. 1 Dock Barry about 1892. Just eight years previously, work began on building the new dock at Barry for the impending increase in coal exports.

Apart from these early mythical sources, historical associations of the Barry area are few. Barry Castle, of which all that remains today are grass-grown remains and an ivy-clad gateway and portcullis, was probably built in the thirteenth century and is known to have been destroyed in a raid by Owain

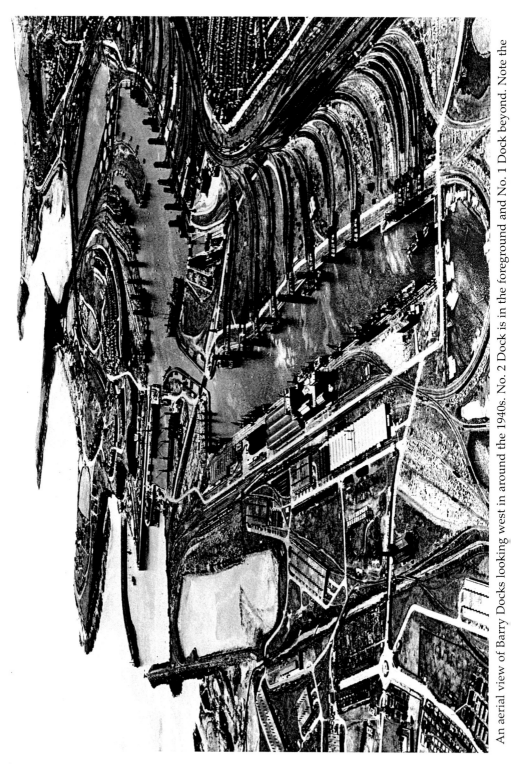

An aerial view of Barry Docks looking west in around the 1940s. No. 2 Dock is in the foreground and No. 1 Dock beyond. Note the

Glerdwr in 1402. Recent archaeological excavations at The Knap have revealed a building of Roman origin, which might have formed part of a base for the Bristol Channel fleet during the Roman occupation of Britain.

In the seventeenth century Barry was used as a refuge and hideout by Bristol Channel pirates and smugglers. In 1734, for instance, vessels engaged on smuggling regularly landed their illicit cargoes at Aberthaw and Barry, and had developed a network of shore-based spies or informers who, after ascertaining the whereabouts of the Customs Officers, would signal to the ships where to land their cargoes. Some 50 years later one Thomas Knight was deeply involved in the smuggling trade. He had ships based on Lundy and Barry Island, and in 1783 descended on Barry with his armed brig together with its 40 men and 24 guns. The only revenue officer in the district was Thomas Hopkins, who did his best against Knight's smugglers and in April 1784 was rewarded with his capture of a quantity of contraband at Barry. Early in 1785 firmer action was taken against Knight's activities at Barry and he was forced to withdraw to his base at Lundy. His place was taken by another notorious smuggler named Arthur, whose presence moved the local law authorities to request the provision of at least 60 soldiers to control the smugglers activities.

The efforts of the Customs and Excise officers eventually succeeded in driving the smugglers away, and it was then possible for law-abiding people to live normal lives in what was still no more than a small coastal village. The first edition (1811) of Carlisle's Topographical Dictionary records that the population of the parish of St. Nicholas, Barry, was 70 people, and the sum raised by the Parish Rates in 1803 amounted to no more than £47 9s 10½d. An impression of Barry Island at that time has been given by the Rev. J Evans who visited Barry in 1803:

'The Island was occupied by numerous colonies of conies, which were taken in large numbers and regularly sent to Bristol and other markets. Quantities of fish frequented the shores, among then the Barry Sole.'

In the early nineteenth century Barry Island was indeed an island, linked to the mainland by a rough ford which could only be traversed by carriages at low tide. The island was mainly agricultural, though it contained one house which during the season could be fitted up as a boarding house for sea bathers of whom 12 could be accommodated at one time. One of the inconveniences of visiting the island at this time was that once there one could only leave it once every 12 hours because the ferry was not fully attended. Such were the beginnings of what was to become the popular seaside resort of modern times!

Although minerals such as lead ore and calamine are said to have been discovered in the limestone of which Barry Island is formed, these deposits played little or no part in the development of Barry as a port. The reason for this, and the real origin of the Barry story from our viewpoint, must be sought elsewhere and in particular in the coal-rich valleys of South Wales some 25 miles distant. Exploitation of this wealth had begun well over 150 years ago and in the next chapter we shall trace the growth of the coal trade which was to bring new life to Barry. For the time being, it is worthy of note that in 1881 the population of Barry still numbered no more than about 500, and that as yet there was but little hint of the great period of growth that was so soon to come.

Chapter Two
HOW COAL CAME TO BARRY

A t the start of Queen Victoria's long reign, a time so closely associated with the formative years of the railway age, the distribution of industry and population in South Wales was very different to that we know today. Before about 1840 the most important ports of the region were Newport, Neath and Swansea, each of them having trading associations of long standing, and sharing the natural advantages of being located near the mouths of major rivers. Barry, as we have already seen, was quite insignificant as a port, while Cardiff - although situated on the River Taff - was but a minor port with very limited wharf accommodation serving the entrance to the Glamorganshire Canal.

By far the most important town of the region was Merthyr Tydfil, which even in 1801 had a population of nearly 8,000 compared to Cardiff's 1,900 and Newport's 1,100. Merthyr was indeed one of the very first centres of the Industrial Revolution and as such deserves our attention, if only briefly, as part of the Barry story. Making use of the local coal and iron ore, a thriving iron industry had become established in and around Merthyr in the early years of the nineteenth century. To serve these industries various early tramroads had been built, among them the famous Penydarren on which Richard Trevithick's pioneering experiments with

steam locomotives were made in 1804. But as yet the main method of transport for the products of the Merthyr ironworks was the Glamorganshire Canal, which had been opened as far as Treforest by 1898 and was subsequently extended up the valley of the Taff to Merthyr itself. The canal was however greatly limited in its capacity to carry both the essential bulk materials such as coal, coke and ore, and the products of the ironworks, by the numerous locks which were needed to raise the level as the canal ascended into the valleys.

Although the tour from which the following description comes was

Statue of David Davies (1818-1890) outside the magnificent headquarters building of the former Barry Railway Company.
M J Beckett

The Barry Railway's viaduct at Walnut Tree was one of the finest in South Wales. Some 130 feet high, it crossed the former Taff Vale line just south of Taffs Well station. Photograph taken in 1965. *M J Beckett*

not made until 1854, it would be difficult to find a more vivid account of the industrial scene in Merthyr than that set down by that indefatigable traveller George Borrow:

'The town is large and populous..........The houses are in general low and mean, and built of rough grey stone. Merthyr, however, can show several remarkable edifices though of a gloomy horrid Satanic character'.

And in relation to the great ironworks at Cyfarthfa Fawr, Borrow wrote:

'I saw enormous furnaces. I saw streams of molten metal. I saw a long ductile piece of red-hot iron being operated upon. I saw millions of sparks flying about. I saw an immense wheel impelled around with frightful velocity by a steam-engine of two hundred and forty horse power. I heard all kinds of dreadful sounds. The general effect was stunning'.

With such activity it was inevitable that the industrial growth in the Merthyr area should attract railways to the district, and in 1836 the Taff Vale Railway Act was passed to authorise the construction of a line from Merthyr to Cardiff. Soon after the Act was passed, and while the line was still under construction, the directors of the Taff Vale Railway opened negotiations with Lord Bute with a view to obtaining access to the latter's new dock which was then being built at Cardiff. This dock, which represented the first stage in the provision of port facilities at Cardiff capable of handling bulk cargoes, was initially described as the Bute Ship Canal. At its landward end, access was provided by a cut linking it to the Glamorganshire Canal, whilst an entrance lock and basin enabled ocean-going ships to use the new dock. Its promotion and construction had been undertaken by Lord Bute at his own expense, and when the dock was eventually opened in October 1839 it had cost him some £400,000. Events were soon to justify such a large investment.

For some years, arrangements for coal shipment were of a temporary nature, but after much negotiation an agreement was concluded between Lord Bute and the Taff Vale Railway, and tipping appliances were erected for the shipment of coal brought down from the valleys by the new line. The combination of improved transport from the mining districts and better shipping facilities at Cardiff brought great success to both the TVR and to Lord Bute's dock, and it was not long before both parties realised the advantages of an arrangement which would protect their interests. In 1849 the dock, which later became known as the Bute West Dock, was leased to the TVR for a period of 250 years, thus in effect creating a monopoly for its proprietors and the railway company. By 1850 some three-quarters of a million tons of coal were being shipped through the Bute West Dock: before its opening the quantity was around 150,000 tons. The seeds of growth had been well and truly sown, but for the TVR the terms of their agreement were to prove restrictive.

In 1848 Lord Bute died, to be succeeded by his infant son, on whose behalf the affairs of the dock interests were being managed by the Bute Trustees who soon decided to proceed with the construction of a second and larger dock. Designs were prepared by Sir John Rennie, and the new dock, which became known as the Bute East, was opened in stages between 1855 and 1859 at a cost of some £500,000. As before, facilities were provided for the shipment of coal, but this time the principal lease went to the Rhymney Railway and not to the Taff Vale, who had to be satisfied with but three berths. In addition the new dock had rail connections to the Great Western Railway which was still operating on Brunel's broad gauge in South Wales.

The Taff Vale Railway had since their agreement with Lord Bute opened new lines in the Aberdare and Rhondda Valleys in order to develop the rich and valuable high quality steam coals of those areas. The steam coals were in great demand for both ships and railway locomotives, each representing forms of transport which were becoming more and more used by both industry and commerce. At the same time as this growth in demand was taking place, economic factors played their part: rising prices at the ports, to some extent stimulated by events such as the Crimean War (1854 -1856) and the 'boom' of 1870-73, all helped to keep the growth continuing ever upward. The years from 1850 to 1880 were thus ones of virtually un-interrupted expansion for the coal export trade of South Wales, but towards the end of this period there were increasing signs that for Cardiff at least the growth in demand was out-stripping the capacity of the port to handle it.

Congestion at Cardiff

The construction of the Bute East Dock had attracted more and more shipping to Cardiff, and congestion at the docks soon followed. In 1856 powers had been obtained to build new docks on the lower reaches of the River Ely at Penarth; these facilities which eventually consisted of both an enclosed dock and a tidal harbour on the river itself, were handling more than a million tons of coal by 1870. Even so, such was the rate of expansion that congestion of another kind - this time

A view of the Bute West Dock, Cardiff, looking towards the basin in about 1860-70. Note the steam paddle tug moored on the left. In the foreground are some of the narrow boats used for transporting bulk freight on the Glamorgan canal which gave direct access to the dock.   *Welsh Industrial & Maritime Museum*

on the railways - began to represent a real problem. In 1870 the Taff Vale line was still the only railway link from the Rhondda pits to the docks at both Cardiff and Penarth, though seriously congested by the much greater volume of coal traffic it now carried. It was not unknown for a train from the Ocean Collieries in the upper Rhondda Valley to take as long as 23 hours on its journey to the Bute Docks, against a schedule of 3½ hours, and it could take just as long to return the empty wagons to the pits. Much of this time was spent standing in sidings waiting for line clearance and access to the docks where the coal was to be shipped. Inevitably on many occasions the pits had to cease production simply because their output of coal could not be loaded and transported away, thus causing loss of revenue for the colliery owners and loss of earnings for the miners.

Throughout the 1870s congestion of both rail and port facilities at Cardiff continued until, by 1880, the Rhondda colliery proprietors were demanding improvements from the Taff Vale Railway and the Bute Trustees. The latter had, by an Act of 1866, obtained powers to build further docks, but apart from the relatively small Roath Basin opened in 1874 they had not provided the expansion so urgently needed. Between 1874 and 1882 the quantities of coal and coke sent to Cardiff increased by well over 200%, and had reached the considerable total of nearly 5 million tons. Almost another 2 million tons were going to Penarth, but even greater tonnages of coal could have been produced had there been adequate facilities to handle them. Such a state of affairs could not long continue, and thus it was that in 1882 the first steps towards lessening the influence of the Bute Trustees and TVR agreement were taken by the coal owners. Led by the redoubtable David Davies, MP for Cardigan Boroughs, whose eventful career had included the building of railways in various parts of Wales before becoming Chairman of the powerful Ocean Collieries Company, a Freighters Committee was formed at Cardiff. Initially the Committee's intention was to consider how the existing facilities could be improved, but encouraged by the promise of assistance from Lord Windsor, who owned land at Barry and was interested in the possibilities for its development, its aims were widened accordingly.

The Battle for Barry

Despite all this, the Bute Trustees had failed to provide the improvements which might have satisfied the coal owners, and matters had reached the stage when in January 1883 for example it was possible to cross from one side of the Bute Dock to the other on the decks of moored ships. When at last it was decided to enlarge from the Roath Basin in 1882, the Trustees sought to finance construction of a new dock by making an additional charge of one penny per ton on all shipments of coal. As far as the coal owners were concerned this was the last straw.

The Freighters Committee now began the process of establishing a completely independent outlet for their coal, and it is important to note that their requirement was not only for port facilities but also for an associated transport system to serve it. After considering an alternative site further west at the mouth of the Ogmore River, Barry was eventually selected. Little time was lost in appointing consulting engineers, and on 30 November 1882 plans for the new dock were laid before Parliament. The survey for the proposed dock site at Barry was undertaken by Mr (later Sir) J Wolfe-Barry assisted by Mr H M Brunel, son of the great Isambard. On 19 December 1882 the Barry Dock and Railway Bill was published and the stage was set for the forthcoming Parliamentary battle to gain approval for the new venture.

When the Bill came before the Commons Committee on 10 April 1883, there was, not unexpectedly, strong opposition from the Taff Vale Railway and the Bute Trustees. However, the arguments put forward by the coal owners carried the day, only for the Bill to be rejected by the Lords in July 1883. Although this was a setback, the promoters were so convinced of the merit of their case that plans were soon prepared for a renewal of the campaign in the next Parliamentary session. In the meantime the Barry promoters offered to purchase the Bute Docks outright and not to proceed with their own scheme until such purchase was completed, but this offer was rejected.

So on 30 April 1884 a Bill differing but slightly from that which had failed in the previous session once again came before a Commons Committee comprising Mr. Foljambe presiding and Messrs Stafford Howard, Northcote and Macartney as members The promoters were represented by Mr Pember QC as chief counsel, but perhaps the most notable legal figure present was Mr Samuel Pope QC, representing the Taff Vale Railway: Mr Pope weighed 20 stones and made legal history by being permitted to conduct his case whilst remaining seated!

Above: Barry Railway class 'J' 2-4-2T No. 88.   *LCGB Ken Nunn collection*

Below: Barry Railway class 'D' 0-8-0 No. 93. These engines were originally built for a Scandinavian railway, but were later re-sold to the Barry Railway and became the first examples of their wheel arrangement on a British Railway.   *LCGB Ken Nunn collection*

The *South Wales Daily News* reported the first day's proceedings in the following terms:

'The proceedings of the opening day appeared to savour very much of the character of a preliminary canter. The legal army whose services have been retained seemed scarcely to have buckled on their armour'.

As the hearings went on the pattern of argument and counter-argument developed much as it had done before. In evidence for the Bill, Mr O H Riches said that if the Taff Vale Railway could get the coal down to the docks as fast as he could walk, he would be satisfied; he could walk at 4 miles per hour. On the difficulties at the Bute Docks, Mr Pember QC had this to say:

'Vessels were now obliged to wait outside, wishing to get in, like Peri at the gates of Paradise, whilst other vessels inside the docks were like rats in a trap, wishing to get out.'

By the time the hearings had reached their thirty-third day all sides and arguments had received full and detailed consideration. It was time for the closing speeches, and much depended on Mr Pember if the ambitions of the Barry Promoters were not again to fail. He was equal to the occasion, for as the South Wales Daily News reported next day:

'Mr Pember's closing speech was a remarkably clever performance..........He spoke for about 3 hours 20 minutes without cessation, excepting an occasional pause to gulp down a tumbler of water, and during the whole of this time there was very little reference to documents.'

'At 4.25 p.m. the Chairman directed the room to be cleared. The corridor opposite No. 4 Room was completely blocked, everyone waiting for the verdict. In about a quarter of an hour's time the doors were opened, There was an excited rush into the room, and before anybody could get seated the Chairman announced that the Committee had approved of the Bill. Many rushed off to the telegraph office at once; the promoters occupied the next few minutes in mutual congratulation.'

This time there was no disappointment when the Bill came before the Lords, for on 31 July 1884 they too passed it, and on 14 August it received Royal Assent. There was now no legal objection to the creation of the new port at Barry together with the railway system linking it to the coalfields, and all that now remained was to raise the necessary capital and carry out the work of construction. The company formed for this purpose had an authorised share capital of £1,050, 000 and was known as the Barry Dock and Railway Company, thus in its title combining the two essential elements of port and transport facilities in a single integrated organisation: the formula that made Barry so different from all previous groupings and one which was to be the key of its success. To quote from the Company's original Prospectus:

'There cannot be the slightest doubt but that the Barry Dock and railways must, as soon as they are opened for traffic, rank with the most prosperous undertakings in the United Kingdom'.

How accurate that prediction was, and just how great was the measure of the success that the new facilities were to achieve, we shall see in a later chapter.

Construction of the dock and railways

Little time was lost by the new company in letting the contracts for construction of the new dock and railways. The successful contractors were:

'Messrs T A Walker: Barry Dock, and the connecting railway as far north as St -y-Nyll

'Lovatt & Shaw: Railway from St -y-Nyll to Treforest

'John Mackay & Son: Railway from Treforest to Hafod Jct.

The total value of these three contracts was estimated at £2,000,000, and to supervise the work the company appointed J Wolfe-Barry, H M Brunel and T Forster Brown as their engineers, assisted by Mr J W Szlumper on the northern section of the railway and by Mr J Robinson as resident engineer at Barry.

On 14 November 1884 at Castleland Point, Lord Windsor as Chairman of the Barry Dock and Railway Company cut the first sod on the site of the future dock. This great undertaking was to require the excavation of some 5 million cubic yards of earth and the building of 200,000 cubic yards of masonry. The task was accomplished by 3,000 men, with over 30 locomotives being used during construction of the dock. The dock was originally planned to have an area of some 40 acres, but during construction an important geological fault was encountered which necessitated the seaward wall of the dock to be set back a considerable distance in order to obtain reliable foundations. As a result, the dock area was enlarged to some 73 acres, making it one of the largest enclosed docks then in existence anywhere in the world. The enlargement provided enough width to allow the provision of a mole at the western end, thus increasing the length of quayside available for berthing of ships. The unusual curved outline of the dock was determined by the nature of the sub-soil, a silty marsh land which marked the course of the former Cadoxton River which used to enter the sea close to Barry Island, before being diverted into a new course as part of the construction works.

The railways also were not without considerable engineering features, which were necessary to provide loaded coal trains being worked down to Barry with as easy a route as possible. This was in general achieved, the maximum ruling gradient against the load being no more severe than 1 in 400, whereas empty trains being worked back to the collieries had to face sections of 1 in 120. Near Wenvoe a tunnel 1 mile 127 yards in length was necessary, and north of Treforest another of some ¾-mile was required; these being the major engineering features of the new line. Since at this stage the main line section of the railway was intended only for mineral traffic, no provision was made for passenger stations. E L Ahrons, who first saw the new line during its construction, records how his companion commented:

'This is going to be 'the' South Wales railway of the future'. On the route itself, Ahrons own comments were perhaps intended to be taken less than seriously:

'The main line strikes north (from Cadoxton) through various places with unpronounceable Welsh names to Hafod Junction............The gentleman who fixed on a place for a railway junction with a name like Tyn-y-caeau ought to have been promptly deported. I have just had three shots at coupling up the vowels in proper order, each one with a worse result than the others!'

The junction in question was the point near St -y-Nyll (itself no easier on non-Welsh tongues!) where connecting lines joined the new Barry main line to the Great Western Railway. Despite such descriptive difficulties, by 22 November 1888 the new main line was sufficiently complete to allow a locomotive to travel over it to reach Barry. Such a momentous occasion did not pass un-noticed, for as the *Barry & Cadoxton Journal* reported:

'On Thursday 22 November the first engine belonging to the Barry Dock & Railway Co. travelled over the line from Pontypridd to Barry. The engine is a powerful one and is coloured chocolate. The most notable part of it is the whistle, which sounds something like the fog whistle of a steamer, and does not at all resemble the sharp shrill whistle of most railway engines'.

Even in those days, it would seem that some press reporters found it difficult to describe anything with which they were not familiar! The engine actually joined Barry metals at Treforest Jct after delivery from its makers at Manchester.

A New Port is Born

The major task was, however, the building of the dock itself, and it was not until 29 June 1889 that the work was sufficiently complete for water to be admitted for the first time. This having been done, preparations were then quickly made for a grand opening ceremony to take place on 18 July 1889. It had taken almost five years from the passage of the Act, but the great day was now in sight. The events of 18 July are perhaps worthy of our attention since they marked the formal commencement of Barry's existence as a commercial port.

As if to reward the promoters for their foresight and patience, the weather for the great occasion could not have been kinder. As the *South Wales Daily News* put it: 'Barry Luck' is a local proverb, 'Barry Weather' must be its latest synonym.'

Invited guests were conveyed in two special trains which left Cardiff at 8.30 a.m. and 8.40 a.m., travelling over the GWR to St. Fagan's where they traversed the connection to Tyn-y-caeau Jct to reach the Barry Company's own metals, then after reversal via Cadoxton to Barry where an improvised platform had been provided close to the dock. Promptly at 9.30 a.m. Miss Barry, daughter of J Wolfe-Barry, operated the lever which opened the outer lock gates of the basin, while a few minutes later the ceremony was repeated at the dock gates themselves with Mrs Brereton performing the task. About an hour later, at 10.30, the S.S. *Arno* of Sunderland, owned by Messrs Westoll and steered on this occasion by T R Thompson of the Barry Company's Board, became the first vessel to enter the new dock. She was followed by many other vessels, including various yachts and pleasure craft in addition to merchant ships, but by 11.30 a.m. coal was being loaded from a consignment of best Rhondda steam coal sent down by Messr; D Davis & Co. of Ferndale.

One slight hiatus to the celebrations occurred at the official luncheon - the waiters went on strike for higher wages! On hearing of this, David Davies advised the guests to help themselves, which they began to do, whereupon the waiters promptly resumed their duties. But Davies had the last say, for at the end of the luncheon he requested, as a special favour, that the guests refrained from tipping the waiters!

The success which the Barry promoters had long predicted was soon confirmed, for almost 40,000 tons of coal were shipped in the first two weeks operation. By the end of the year, nearly 600 ships and more than one million tons of coal had been loaded, and Barry had been launched on the astonishing rise which was eventually to see it become one of the greatest coal-exporting ports in Britain.

David Davies lived for barely a year after the great opening day, and in September 1889 he addressed the Barry shareholders in what was to prove the last major speech of his eventful life:

'We have finished a work which might well be called gigantic; we have done it well and cheaply; we have not wasted any of your money................Do not be afraid that the Taff and the Bute people are going to run us to ground. They will run themselves to ground first, and they know it by this time!'

He died on 20 July 1890, having seen his creation of the new port of Barry reach fruition, and is commemorated in the form of a life-sized statue in bronze which stands to this day outside the magnificent headquarters building which the Barry Company built in 1898 to house their thriving and prosperous business.

Wagons of many private colliery companies stand in the sidings near Barry Works, seen in the right background of this 1926 photograph. On the left, one of the power plants serving the docks hydraulic system can be seen. The two curved inclined sidings immediately in front of the buildings were used for storage of condemned locomotives after purchase by Woodham Brothers from 1964 onwards. *BR Western Region*

Chapter Three
GROWTH AND ACHIEVEMENT

The initial success of the new port was no short-lived phenomenon, for the first quarter-century of Barry's operation was a period of remarkable expansion, which in intensity has rarely been equalled in Britain before or since. This success was demonstrated in both the quantities of coal exported and in the steady increase in the population of the new town. To deal first with the coal trade, the consequences of the opening of the new dock were immediate: some 60% of Penarth's traffic was quickly attracted to Barry, while the Taff Vale Railway was compelled to reduce its own rates for carriage of coal to an extent which used its gross revenue to decrease from almost £890,000 to around £710,000 between 1888 and 1890. As a result the dividend paid on TVR ordinary shares was cut from 15% to 7½%, even though the railway was being subsidised to the extent of £30,000 p.a. by the Bute Dock Company.

At Barry, however, the first 10 years saw continued growth as will be seen from the following table:

Year	Number of ships	Coal/coke exports (tons)
1889 (5 months)	598	1.07 million
1890	1753	3.19
1891	2096	3.96
1892	2182	4.19
1893 (strike)	2162	4.21
1894	2166	4.89
1895	2278	5.05
1896	2646	5.28
1897	2806	5.85
1898 (strike)	2271	4.37

It was not long before the need for a second dock became apparent, and by an Act of 1893 the Company obtained powers to build it; the dock was opened in 1898 and provided another 34 acres of enclosed water. Another decision taken during these early years saw the Company changing its name to the simpler 'Barry Railway Company' by which it was known for the remainder of its independent existence.

It was inevitable that commercial success brought with it rapid change to the former small coastal settlement of Barry. Within two years of the opening, the population had risen to more than 12,000, and by 1901 there were some 27,000 inhabitants: in 1881 there were only about 500! Although most of this great increase was represented by Barry itself, at the same time the adjoining and previously isolated Island was beginning to he developed as a popular holiday resort.

An impression of these years of such rapid growth is contained in a little publication 'Where are you going for your holiday' from the Barry Chamber of Trade and Improvement, and dates from July 1897. In the proper and correct language of its time, this little booklet vividly conveys the satisfaction and pride felt by Barry's inhabitants in their fine new town:

'Because Barry exports more than 5 million tons of coal a year it must not therefore be concluded that it is bounded on the north, south, east and west by coal tips. The town and district have features of great interest and value quite outside the unique, we may say the unparalleled success, of its Dock Undertaking'.

'Can any good come out of Barry except 10% dividends? will become a more and more impossible question, for what the Mumbles and Langland Bay are to Swansea, Barry is certainly destined to be to Cardiff and the teeming Hill Districts - on a recent Bank Holiday over 25,000 people visited the town.....................

Among the attractions offered to those crowds of visitors, the following are some examples taken from the booklet:

'Hurley's Jubilee Tea and Coffee Room, Romilly Buildings (opposite station): A large selection of choice fruits, sweets and chocolates always in stock.'

'Sea View Restaurant, 5 Barry Dock Road: Proprietress M A Jones. First class accommodation. Hot and cold baths. Well aired beds from one shilling. London and daily papers'.

'The Universal Restaurant, Island Road, Barry: Proprietor T J Radcliffe. Hot dinners daily from 12.30 to 2.00, 6d, 9d and 1s.

While at the **'Barry Supply Stores'**, 92 High Street, the following 'well known articles' were on sale:

Dr. Tibbles Vi-Cocoa
Harris & Co's. Celebrated Wiltshire smoked bacon
Palethorpe's Royal Cambridge Sausages
Prices' Patent Night Lights and Candles
Maypole Soap for dyeing Etc.

One wonders what magic names are covered by that all-embracing 'Etc'! It is also possible to note perhaps the first appearance of a Barry name destined to become familiar in our own times:

'S Woodham & Son', 108 High St and 1 Bell St, Barry:
Fish, fruit, potato, poultry etc.
General Hauliers
Furniture removals and warehousing
Cabs and Brakes, Horses etc for hire.'

S. Woodham was the great-uncle of Mr Dai Woodham, proprietor of Woodham Bros. Ltd. A 6-roomed cottage in Spencer Street near Barry Dock station could be bought for £160, while in nearby Hunter Street a corner house and shop, with adjacent cottage, was on offer at £775.

The new town had 10 daily despatches of mail from 5.15 a.m. until 9.0 p.m., while 5 deliveries were made from 7.30 a.m. until 8.0 p.m. Unsocial hours had not been invented in those days!

Since August 1893 the Barry Company had been operating its own passenger trains from Barry to Cardiff, using running powers over the TVR from Cogan Junction and over the GWR's Riverside Branch in Cardiff itself. By 1897 the service comprised some 18 trains per day in each direction, and a growing commuter traffic was developing. In other directions too the railway's passenger traffic was expanding, since from March 1896 the company's main line had been carrying passenger trains between Barry and Porth in the Rhondda Valley, with new stations being provided at some of those unpronounceable places remarked on by Ahrons: Wenvoe, Creigiau, Efail Isaf, Treforest and Pontypridd. The line had not been built with passenger trains in mind, but the growing popularity of Barry Island as a seaside resort led to demands from the Rhondda mining communities for direct rail access to Barry. Before their wishes could be fulfilled, the Company had to provide additional signalling and other necessary safety measures to satisfy the Board of Trade's requirements, but when the Inspecting Officer Col. H A Yorke carried out the statutory examination he was able to report:

'The rails show little signs of wear despite being in use for mineral traffic for seven years, and the permanent way is in first class order'.

An excellent confirmation of the high standards to which the line had been designed and constructed. Even so, the regulations for working the line included the rule that no mineral train was to be allowed to proceed in front of a passenger train with less than a 10-minute margin before the departure of the latter. Although the service between Barry and Porth never reached the intensity of the Cardiff trains, the line came into its own for excursion traffic, especially during the summer and on public holidays when Barry Island was the choice of many thousands of visitors who travelled on the numerous specials arranged by choirs, miners welfare parties, Sunday schools, and many other organisations.

But the real wealth of the Barry Railway was always its coal traffic, and during the 25 years which followed the opening of the port the Company made great efforts to attract further traffic to their line. There were many attempts, with varying degrees of success, to expand the system over these years, and they gained for the Barry Railway the reputation of having somewhat uncompromising ambitions. At first, however, all went well, for in 1897 an agreement was reached with the nominally independent Vale of Glamorgan Railway whose line connected Barry with Bridgend via a coastal route some 20 miles in length. This line carried both passenger and freight traffic, though the latter never reached the levels which the Barry had expected. Better results in this respect were achieved from the successive extensions authorised in 1896 and 1898 which saw new lines linking first the Rhymney and later the Brecon & Merthyr, railways to the Barry's own metals at Tyn-y-caeau Junction. These extensions required some of the most substantial viaducts on any South Wales railway, with these at Taffs Well and Llanbradach being the best know. It is a measure of the very extensive engineering works involved on both these lines that their construction required 5 and 7 years respectively from the passage of the two Acts concerned.

Among the schemes which never reached fruition, the most intriguing was without doubt the 1895 proposal for a new trunk main line from South Wales to London. After the passage of so many years it is now difficult to establish exactly to what extent the Barry Railway were behind the scheme, but it is certain that at the very least they were active supporters of it. In addition to assisting with the

One of the last two tipping hoists at No. 1 Dock in 1979. Despite appearances the small coaster alongside the tip is not loading coal.

In 1939 the GWR announced that there were 29 of these appliances, 18 of which were capable of handling 20-ton wagon loads.
M J Beckett

legal costs of the London & South Wales Railway Bill, Barry Railway personalities including Lord Windsor and Sir John Wolfe-Barry were proposed as directors of the new company. The scheme was an ambitious one involving the construction of some 160 miles of main line railway which would have required crossing the River Seven by a bridge having a total length of 3300 yards, and two tunnels of about 2500 yards to carry the line through the Cotswolds. At the London end access to the capital would have been achieved through running powers over the lines of an existing company, and at various times the Metropolitan and the Midland were regarded as likely hosts to the new concern. In South Wales a westward extension of the Vale of Glamorgan Railway would have carried the L & S W towards Swansea. In all these possible combinations the Barry Company would have been well placed to benefit by the additional freight and passenger traffic which the promoters hoped to win. There are however strong indications that the real motive behind the Bill was to obtain further concessions from the Great Western, with particular regard to the rates for coal traffic being developed at Barry and the improvement of the GWR's routes to South Wales. The outcome was that the Bill was withdrawn by its promoters following negotiations with the GWR Board. Perhaps the best description of the whole scheme was that given by the London correspondent of the *Western Mail*, whose report of the agreement with the GWR appeared on 14 January 1896 under the fitting headline: 'That Ephemeral Main Line'.

Although the line was never built and today seems perhaps totally unrealistic, it provides us with an excellent illustration of the undoubted ambition and commercial potential that was stimulated by the success of Barry as a port and railway centre A further example was the attempt to run passenger steamer services between Barry and other South Wales ports and across the Bristol Channel to Devon and Somerset. Once again the Barry Railway took the lead, and services actually commenced in 1905 between Barry Pier, Weston-super-mare and Ilfracombe. By 1907 a fleet of four vessels was operating excursions, pleasure cruises and limited cargo traffic, but because of strong opposition from other operators and the strict conditions set by the powers granted to the Barry company these services were never financially successful. After trying valiantly to overcome these constraints, the Barry had in 1910 to admit defeat and the four steamers were sold, three of them eventually coming into the ownership of Messrs P & A Campbell Ltd who had been among the principal opponents of the venture. After serving their new owners throughout the inter-war period these three ships were all lost in the early years of the last war, though not before rendering valuable service in the Dunkirk evacuations.

Despite these setbacks and frustrations the continued growth of the coal export trade made the Barry a sound and successful concern, and its shareholders could look forward to regular dividends of around 10% in most years, though this did not prevent them from frequently expressing criticism of the Board over such matters as the failure of the steamer services. But by 1913 even the sternest critics must have found satisfaction in their Company's achievements, for in that year Barry exported some 11 ¾ million tons of coal - the largest annual tonnage ever handled by any single port engaged on this trade.

Not without reason could South Wales claim to be the 'coal capital of the world'! Over 50% of the annual output of the South Wales coalfield was exported with France, South America, Italy, Egypt and Spain usually being the largest customers. The trade was indeed world-wide, for along all the principal maritime routes chains of coaling stations supplied with best Welsh steam coal were established.

Speed and efficiency were essential requirements of the ports through which such large amounts of coal passed. At Barry the docks were provided with 45 hydraulically powered hoists which when operating at their maximum rate could load vessels at up to 600 tons per hour, though in normal use the rate of loading was much smaller. The coaling appliances at Barry were approached by inclined ramps leading from the reception and sorting sidings, and in all there were more than 100 miles of siding accommodation in the Barry area. Loaded trains were worked down from the collieries to the reception sidings, where they were sorted into groups according to the quality or origin of each type of coal by a different locomotive from that used for the main line haulage. Shipments of coal could be specified either of one type or be of mixed groups, the latter being the cargoes most often required by the exporters. Mixed cargoes required further shunting, and additional engines had to be available for such work, so that the dock area was constantly alive with locomotive and wagon movements in all directions. The layout at Barry was well suited to such activity, and represented a great improvement over the older and less spacious accommodation at the Bute Docks. Inevitably with such intensive operations accidents of various sorts occurred, though in this respect Barry's record was no worse than that of any other similar port. One of the more spectacular accidents occurred in 1908, when the S.S. *Walkure* was coaling alongside No.2 Dock. At some stage her cargo of timber and pitwood became unstable, causing the ship to list seriously to port until it came to rest against the dock floor with substantial damage to the ship's superstructure. No loss of life occurred and the vessel was successfully righted with the assistance of the Barry Railway's powerful 8-coupled tank engines.

In so many ways, 1914 marked the end of an era both for Barry and for the trade which had created it. Coal was still in great demand, but the needs of war brought other traffic in increasing quantities. During the war Barry dealt with over 6,000 Admiralty and 300 military shipping movements, including the embarkation of troops and their equipment. One of the decisions made during the wartime period was to place all railway companies under the overall control of a Railway Executive responsible to the Government. Although this represented the first step towards eventual state control of the nation's railways, in the event full nationalisation was not adopted when the war ended in 1918. Instead, companies were to be combined in four major groups, and for the Barry Railway this meant absorption into the GWR.

The interior of Barry works on 8th May 1959. Locomotives visible include Nos. 5641, 6644 (centre) and 5687. Beyond 6644 is 0-6-0PT No. 9714. This was the final year of overhauls of locomotives at Barry works. After a few years repairing wagons, it was finally closed in 1965 and demolished soon afterwards. *E R Mountford*

Chapter Four
DIFFICULT TIMES

The Great Western takes over

Although the Railway Grouping is usually regarded as having taken place in 1923, for the Barry Railway and for several other constituents of the enlarged GWR their independent existence ended in theory at the end of 1921. In practice, amalgamation of the BR and GWR did not take place until 8 May 1922. In its final years the Barry company had maintained its fine record of achievement and profitability, with 10% dividends and increased total assets in each of its last three years. So the Great Western inherited no 'lame duck' when it took over at Barry, and though the coal trade was never to reach its pre-war levels it was at first still extremely substantial. It was as well that this was so, for the GWR had inherited from its South Wales absorbed companies a system of docks and railways which had been designed with competition in mind, and where co-operation was decidedly a secondary objective. Together with the LNER Group, the Great Western had been placed in the position of being the largest dock owning concern in Britain, and was therefore in a good position to carry out such rationalisation as it thought fit and necessary.

On Grouping, the Barry Railway's Chairman, the Earl of Plymouth (Lord Windsor) was elected to the GWR Board, while the Barry's former General Manager and Locomotive Engineer filled posts in the Docks Department. With these positions held by its former servants, the Barry interests might have hoped to survive the rigours of the changed situation relatively comfortably, and so it might have proved had not the decline in the coal export trade continued and reached alarming proportions. Between 1920 and 1924 coal exports had actually increased from 7.4 to 9.1 million tons, but thereafter a steady decrease set in which was made worse by the General Strike of 1926 and the later years of depression in the 1930s, until by 1938 only 5.4 million tons passed through Barry. The reasons for this decline, which was not restricted just to Barry or even to all of the South Wales coal ports, undoubtedly stemmed from the change in world trading patterns brought about by the Great War, though in addition newer methods of marine propulsion were making inroads into the supremacy of steam.

One of the first casualties of the decline in traffic was the Barry's last and greatest extension line, that linking it to the Brecon and Merthyr Railway. With all the erstwhile competing railways now under single command there was considerable scope for elimination of former Barry routes, whose traffic was not only much smaller than before but could be diverted to its originating lines quite easily.

With its long viaducts the Barry's B&M extension was more costly to maintain than the other routes, and so in 1926 the GWR obtained powers to abandon surplus lines which included the B&M link. The great viaducts were not immediately demolished, and in fact were to survive until 1937 having seen barely 30 years existence. From 1930 the Barry-Porth passenger trains were rerouted from

Tonteg Jct. to run via Treforest and thence over the ex-Taff Vale line to terminate at Pontypridd, thus allowing the closure of the Barry's station at the latter place.

The GWR also introduced its own range of standard locomotive types in place of the multiplicity of classes handed over by its constituents.

For the heavier duties this meant a return to the use of eight-coupled tank locomotives of the 42XX and later the 72XX classes, while a new class of 0-6-2 tanks was introduced with mixed traffic work particularly in mind. It was this class (56XX) which replaced many of the older locomotives of the same wheel arrangement used by so many of the South Wales railways. Several former Barry Railway engines were sold out of GWR service following these changes, and thereby were in some cases to enjoy lives longer by many years than their fellows which had remained in Great Western ownership.

By the mid-1930s there was considerable surplus dock capacity available for coal traffic, and in addition some of the older docks were needing substantial expenditure for replacement of life-expired equipment. This was to mean the closure of Penarth for coal shipments, while at Cardiff coal traffic was to be increasingly concentrated on the more recent docks, though coal continued to be shipped from both the Bute Docks until post-war times. Barry was however retained as a major outlet for coal, and the GWR invested large sums to modernise the coaling appliances. Indeed, when on 14 November 1934 the Great Western commemorated the 50th anniversary of the cutting of the first sod at Barry Docks

Many Barry Railway locomotives were sold out of GWR service and several were purchased by collieries in the north-east of England. GWR No. 729 (formerly Barry Railway No. 130) is seen here at North Walbottle Colliery, Northumberland in 1961.

R G Farr

by holding a special dinner for over 300 members of the former Barry Company's staff, Lord Davies (grandson of the port's founder) looked forward to regaining much of the trade that had been lost, but sadly his optimism was not to be realised. Towards the end of the inter-war period the quantities of coal exported were down to around 5 million tons, less than half the peak annual rate of the pre-1914 years. A start had however been made in attracting new traffic to the port, and although in only small quantities commodities such as foodstuffs, timber, grain and manufactured goods had been added to Barry's trade.

At the commencement of hostilities in 1939 official policy was to make greater use of ports on the western coasts of Britain, as they were thought less susceptible to attack from the air or by surface ships and mines than the major ports on the east and south coasts from the Tyne to the Solent. Among the most important tasks assigned to the South Wales ports was coal movement, not only for the home market but in particular to ensure that adequate supplies continued to reach France, whose usual peacetime sources were no longer available. All these factors resulted in a much greater demand being placed on the railway systems serving the South Wales ports, and in particular their links with the main centres of population and demand in the remainder of Britain. The situation became extremely serious after the fall of France in mid-1940, since there were then considerable quantities of surplus coal which could not be used locally and could only very slowly be moved out of South Wales to area of greater demand. The major limiting factor was the line capacity of the GWR's Severn Tunnel route: whereas a passenger train could pass through the tunnel in 6 minutes, a coal train needed 15 and in addition required the use of assistant engines. One wonders if the decision not to build the London & South Wales line might not have been a mistake after all, but in the difficult circumstances of the time no such solution could be considered. Instead, improvements were made to increase the traffic capacities of the Newport - Severn Tunnel section and the line from Newport to Hereford and Shrewsbury, which together with the introduction of Sunday working via the Severn Tunnel provided temporary relief. At Cardiff and Barry further siding accommodation was provided, and slowly the situation improved until the next crisis developed; this being a shortage of adequate locomotive power. This in turn was remedied by the construction of large numbers of 2-8-0 freight engines to the LMS Stanier design and the Wartime 'Austerity' pattern, together with the temporary assistance of USATC S-160 2-8-0s from 1943 onwards. Whilst awaiting shipment to Europe, many of the American engines saw service on GWR lines and others were stored on former Barry metals at Cadoxton, Penrhos and Treforest.

Although the railway system was under pressure for almost the whole wartime period, coastal shipment of coal could for much of the time proceed with relatively little disruption, and this provided some slight relief to the problems of the railway network. This was not always the case however, for in mid-1942 a small convoy of 10 ships sailing from Barry with coal for Southampton was attacked by E-boats; only two vessels, loaded with survivors, completed the voyage.

In addition to the coal traffic which was handled during the war years, general military and naval shipping was also dealt with, and Barry was particularly used by the American forces in the latter part of the period.

When the war ended a slow return to the commercial traffic patterns of the 1930s began, but before this had progressed very far another major change in ownership was initiated by the Transport Act of 1947. This provided for the full nationalisation of the railway groups and their dock undertakings under the control of the British Transport Commission, the former GWR becoming the Western Region of British Railways while the major South Wales ports were grouped under a Chief Docks Manager based at Cardiff. Ironically the headquarters of the new Docks Manager were in the building of the former Bute Docks Company, so that Barry had at last been brought under the control of an administration housed in the premises of its one-time principal rival. But the problems and challenges facing the nationalised transport industries were such that thoughts of a competitive nature could not be entertained.

Nationalisation comes to Barry

Although coal exports had resumed after the war, they were on such a small scale as to be insignificant compared to the hey-day of pre-1914 times. This was true not merely in South Wales, but of all the U.K. ports which had at one time had a sizeable coal export trade:

TOTAL EXPORTS (in millions of tons)

	1923	1929	1938	1960
Coal, coke and manufactured fuels	83.5	63.2	37.8	6.8
Bunker coal	18.1	16.4	10.5	0.3
Total shipments	101.6	79.6	48.3	7.1

With barely 7 million tons being exported by all ports in total, the measure of the decline can be well appreciated. Individually, the South Wales coal ports were operating at a fraction of their potential capacity: by the closing years of the 1950s, Barry for example was handling less than 1 million tons per year. The former trade pattern of 'coal out, grain in' had disappeared completely, and with it the familiar all-purpose ocean going tramp steamer on which the trade had been based. Post-war conditions favoured larger special-purpose ships such as oil tankers and ore carriers, and in more recent years container ships. The former railway-owned coal ports were at a considerable disadvantage when it came to attracting such vessels, because the size and depth of the docks were often too restrictive to make access possible.

But although Barry's days as a major coal port had gone, considerable progress had been made in attracting other traffic. A large oil storage installation was built at the western end of No. 1 Dock, partly using the mole which had been provided when the width of the dock was increased. At No.2 Dock, facilities for the import of grain, flour, foodstuffs and fruit were developed, with bananas becoming an increasingly important traffic from 1956 onwards. At Sully a large petrochemical plant was built on land close to the dock areas. Thus by 1959, although the total traffic through the port amounted to only around 1.2 million tons, Barry was far less dependent on coal than before, and this trend was to continue.

The transition from dependence on coal to the multi-purpose port of modern times was a long and difficult process, and would have been even more painful had the resources and control provided by the BTC not been available. Being a much larger undertaking, the BTC could and did devote considerable effort to modernising and re-equipping the former coal ports of South Wales, the intention being that each individual port would develop within an integrated structure whilst specialising in particular traffics, such as the deep water iron-ore terminal built at Port Talbot. Coal exports were to be concentrated on Barry and Swansea, and some of the coaling appliances at Barry were modernised at considerable cost. Redundant coal shipping installations at Newport, Cardiff and Barry were to be removed and the berths converted to handle a much wider range of general cargoes. These developments could not be expected to produce results immediately, but it was an encouraging sign that the policies were succeeding that in 1961, for the first time since the war, each of the South Wales ports showed an operating profit.

In 1962, however, came a setback, which as far as Barry was concerned must at the time have been a considerable shock. This was the publication of the report of Lord Rochdale's Committee of Inquiry into the major ports of Great Britain. Noting especially the overwhelming and continuing decline in coal exports, the Committee concluded that there was excessive surplus capacity in the ports and recommended that the trade of Barry Docks should be transferred to Cardiff with a view to the eventual closure of Barry. The next year saw the transfer of the BTC Docks to the newly established British Transport Docks Board, who fortunately reprieved Barry from the fate prescribed by the Rochdale Committee, and instead resumed the process of investment and modernisation. Among the factors which had contributed to the decision not to close Barry were the recent encouraging increases in the oil, grain and banana traffic together with the limited coal trade that had been retained even in the difficult times of the 1960s.

On the railway side, however, Barry fared less well under British Railways control. This was particularly marked in the case of freight traffic, for it was this above all else that Barry's railways depended. Unfortunately the general decline in bulk haulage of coal and minerals resulted in a considerable surplus of capacity both in routes and rolling stock, which in the case of Barry was not balanced by a growth in other rail traffic. In the years immediately following the British Railways Modernisation Plan of 1955, a substantial reduction in the stock of freight wagons formerly used for coal traffic was made, many of these vehicles being broken up in the Barry area.

By the end of the 1950s overhaul of steam locomotives had ceased at Barry, the last engine to be repaired there leaving the works on Christmas Eve of 1959. For a year or two the works was retained for wagon repairs, but by 1965 these too had ceased and the buildings were then demolished. Another casualty during this period was the closure of the former Barry Railway main line from Cadoxton to Tonteg Jct. and Treforest, following the destruction by fire of Tynycaeau Jct. signal box in March 1963. The line was lifted some two years later, and marked the end of the great enterprise which had begun so notably almost 80 years before. Amidst these gloomy occurrences the continued popularity of Barry Island as a seaside resort, and the usefulness of the Vale of Glamorgan line as a diversionary route, have ensured that Barry has retained at least some of its former railway importance. The South Wales tradition of day excursions to the seaside soon resumed after the war, and brought a wide variety of locomotives to Barry. From destinations once served by the LMS came ex-LNWR 0-8-0s from Abergavenny and Tredegar sheds with well-filled trains of non-corridor stock, and after their passengers had been safely delivered to Barry Island's beaches the 0-8-0s would shuffle round a tortuous circuit formed by the dock lines in order to turn. None of the larger ex-GWR tender classes was allowed a similar facility, so turning of 'Halls', 'Castles' and other 4-6-0 types used on excursions from London, the West Midlands and elsewhere required much light engine mileage to and from Cardiff. Suburban trains from Barry to Cardiff and the Valleys remained steam-hauled until the late 1950s. These trains provided some of the last duties for ex-Taff Vale Rly 0-6-2Ts, which lasted as late as 1957 on working of this type. In addition, ex-GWR 0-6-2 and 2-6-2 tank types could be found until finally displaced by diesel multiple units in the late 1950s.

The modern port
There have been no further changes in control of the port since 1963, and Barry now forms part of the South Wales region of the British Transport Docks Board. The Board's local office at Barry is located in the still impressive headquarters building which the Barry Company opened in 1898, thus providing continuity with the far-sighted men whose enterprise gave birth to the port almost a century ago. Yet if David Davies could return to the Barry of the present day, how changed he would find the scene at the docks over which his statue still presides! Gone now the coal tipping hoists, with their row upon row of loaded wagons containing best steam coal for shipment. In their place, he would see modernised quays and dockside installations handling a wide range of goods: bananas, grain and flour, chemicals, fuel oils among them. All that remains of the once mighty coal trade is a new mechanised conveyor system opened by the BTBD in 1978 to provide the much smaller capacity needed in the 1980s. What indeed would 'Davies The Ocean' think if by chance his eye should turn westwards, where beyond No.1 Dock stand the last descendants of the hard-working locomotives which once brought down those millions of tons of coal from his Rhondda mines? Their survival, and in many cases their resurrection, has brought the name of Barry once again to the public's attention in a new and unique way, as we shall now see.

A lasting reminder of the old railway and docks owned by the Barry Railway Company. The headquarters building remains today and towers over the new developments on the waterfront area.

Chapter Five
A NEW ROLE FOR BARRY

We come now to the events which have brought the name of Barry once more into prominence, and which have earned it fame in a way so very different from anything in its previous railway history. Indeed, the upsurge of interest in Barry is a unique phenomenon as far as the railway enthusiast fraternity is concerned - yet not only are railway enthusiasts involved, but a large cross-section of public opinion, which even extended to the House of Commons! More than one Parliamentary Question was framed on the subject of the locomotives at Barry, so the study of the origins and subsequent developments affecting them deserves our serious attention.

The Death Sentence for Steam

A convenient starting point is provided for our present purposes by the announcement in 1955 of the Modernisation Plan for British Railways. Until then, the position of steam as the prime mover on the nationalised railways was virtually unchallenged, apart from a handful of main line diesel locomotives, a somewhat larger number of diesel shunters, and the suburban electrification schemes bequeathed by three of the "Big Four" companies - the Great Western being the exception. The 1955 Plan, however, envisaged far-reaching changes in railway motive power, besides other important developments, and its most relevant proposals as far as the Barry story is concerned were:

1. Replacement of steam locomotives by diesel and electric traction.
2. Modernisation of rolling stock, and in particular the replacement of many older freight vehicles of low capacity formerly operated by private owners.

The 1955 Modernisation Plan, announced at an estimated cost of £250m, had as its main objectives the reduction of the BR wagon fleet by around 50% from its then total of 1.25 million vehicles and the elimination of steam traction from main line use by diesels and electrics.

Reduction of the wagon fleet was particularly important. These vehicles were mostly 4-wheeled, loose-coupled open wagons for coal and mineral traffic, many of them wooden-bodied vehicles inherited from former private owners. Their value in terms of productivity was particularly poor. These old wagons were achieving no more than one revenue-earning journey per week, the rest of their time was spent being unloaded and returned to colliery sidings for reloading. Train speeds were low, being influenced by braking power and line capacity. It was becoming essential, if the objective of speeding up services was to be achieved, to reduce the occupation of important routes by these slow-moving mineral trains.

At about the same time (1956) BR still operated, and was largely dependent on, almost 16,000 steam locomotives. As yet, diesel and electric traction had made little input on motive power provision.

Above: One of the businesses of Woodham Brothers involved salvage from all types of dock operations. Here a lorry full of rope recovered from ships in the port has been reclaimed and is soon to be on its way to another customer.

Below: One of the tip lines in No. 2 dock used by Woodhams to dispose of old wagons in the late 1950s. Planks from wooden-bodied wagons are recovered for use elsewhere and are seen strewn on the embankment below.   *Woodham family collection*

A 'sea' of locomotives at Barry in 1969. Billy Woodham, who sadly died soon afterwards, was responsible with Dai Woodham for the accumulation of locomotives in the yards.

Under the Modernisation Plan, it was decided to accelerate the ordering of diesel locomotives for main line duties and to put more than 500,000 redundant wagons out to tender to be scrapped by private contractors.

Woodhams were one of the scrap dealers invited to take part in this disposal scheme. The company was a family-owned business which had been connected with the port of Barry since within a few years of coal traffic beginning. By the mid-1950s it was headed by the founder's youngest son D.L.V. (Dai) Woodham and its range of operations included many port-related activities, transport and haulage and dealing in scrap metals.

Woodhams began cutting up redundant wagons in 1957 and this soon developed into a regular part of their business.

By the late 1950s, BR was finding that the rate at which steam locomotives were being withdrawn was beginning to outstrip the capacity available at BR workshops to break them up and dismantle them. This led to dumps of withdrawn locomotives accumulating at and around principal BR locomotive workshops. This trend was especially noticeable in and around Swindon Works, the Western Region's principal location for scrapping, overhauling and construction of new locomotives.

Woodhams and other scrap dealers began to approach BR WR requesting that they could become involved in the disposal of redundant locomotives, as they had in the case of surplus wagon and rolling stock. The Western Region had a somewhat traditionalist view of motive power requirements and several of its principal locomotive designs were beginning to appear dated compared to developments on other regions of BR. For example, new builds of 'Castle' and 'Manor' class 4-6-0s were constructed at Swindon into the 1950s and two new designs of 0-6-0 pannier tanks were also introduced after the formation of BR in 1948. Besides these, substantial numbers of new pannier tanks were ordered from private locomotive builders and deliveries of these continued well into the 1950s, despite the introduction of new 350hp diesel-electric shunters for broadly similar duties at the same time.

All this meant that the WR was well stocked with locomotives of relatively recent construction for which the traffic requirement was diminishing. Thus, by early 1959, Woodham Brothers became involved in the disposal of surplus steam locomotives from Swindon Works, and on extension of their continuing involvement with the breaking up of wagons.

The firm acquired its first locomotives for breaking up in March 1959: four 43XX 2-6-0 Moguls and one 2-6-2T (No. 3170) all of which were more or less life-expired having completed 40 years of service. At this time Woodham Brothers were operating from leased siding accommodation near Barry Works. The larger amounts of space available on the West Pond site and in the adjacent low-level sidings near the oil terminal were not at this stage rented.

Matters continued on this basis for 2-3 years until a significant expansion took place in 1960 with the acquisition of 40 withdrawn locomotives from Swindon. To accommodate numbers on that scale it was found necessary to begin storing locomotives in the low-level sidings until they could be broken up in the scrapping area located on the West Pond site.

Further acquisitions on a smaller scale continued for the next 2-3 years until by 1964 the purchase of locomotives began from the Southern Region as well as continuing from the Western Region.

Throughout these early years of locomotive acquisitions at Barry, the company continued to be fully occupied with the wagon dismantling contracts, with the result that the Barry Docks area accumulated a large collection of both wagons and locomotives. In order to achieve a faster rate of return on investment, Woodham Brothers decided in 1965 to concentrate their activities on the disposal of wagons and rolling stock. These could be broken up more rapidly than locomotives, thus yielding a quicker return on the financial outlay which the firm had invested in purchasing the locomotives. It must be remembered that this was a multi-million pound business. Acquisition of locomotives did not entirely cease and most of those bought after 1965 were acquired from areas farther away from Barry including parts of the London Midland Region.

By the late 1960s, when many of the other scrap dealers who had taken part in the disposal of BR's 16,000 steam locomotives had finished their acquisitions, at Barry Woodham Brothers were still busily engaged in disposal of wagons and in addition had built up a collection of more than 200 locomotives. It was their intention to dismantle these when the wagon contacts ceased.

At this stage, with BR steam traction within sight of its planned end in the summer of 1968, interest in the collection of locomotives at Barry began to attract attention from the embryo preservation movement.

Part of the old West Pond site after reclamation in the 1950s. The old sidings curving away on the right would be full of redundant locomotives 10 years later. The few sidings in the top centre would become the cutting up areas firstly used by J O Williams Ltd in the late 1950s and then later Woodham Brothers. *ABP*

A Problem Of Space

On the Western Region the availability of new diesel shunters and d.m.us. under the Modernisation Plan had an immediate effect in the displacement of large numbers of steam tank locomotives, a generic type with which the WR was especially well endowed. Among the classes thus affected were the various types of ex-GWR 0-6-0PT and 2-6-2T engines, many of which were of comparatively recent construction - indeed the final deliveries of engines in the '34XX' series had still to be made when the Modernisation Plan was announced. At the same time, older locomotives such as the Churchward 2-6-0 and 2-8-0 classes were being withdrawn on completing their normal life expectancies.

In the mid-1950s it was normal practice on the WR to send condemned engines, after withdrawal from their home sheds, to a main works for breaking up. Being the largest of the Regions works, Swindon dealt with most of the withdrawn engines, but small numbers were sent to Caerphilly and Wolverhampton. The smaller WR works such as Barry and Newton Abbot rarely scrapped locomotives.

After reaching Swindon, a condemned engine would normally be broken up within 2-3 months of withdrawal, scrapping taking place in 'C' shop at the western end of the works site. The capacity of 'C' shop was normally of the order of 2-3 locomotives per week, and this was quite adequate to deal with the rate of withdrawals in normal times. But from 1958 onwards, as the steam replacement programme gathered pace, the capacity of 'C' shop began to be an important limitation. Withdrawn engines were taking longer and longer to be broken up, and it became necessary to store them pending their turn for scrapping in the sidings adjacent to 'C' shop. This area - known as 'The Dump' - presented the appearance so familiar from photographs of the period following the end of the broad gauge in 1892, with long lines of condemned engines forlornly awaiting their fate, and from 1958 similar scenes could once again be recorded. Once the storage capacity of 'The Dump' was filled, other places in and around the works began to be used, notably the 'Stock Shed' and 'Gasworks Yard' close to Swindon (82C) running shed. The locomotives stored in the latter yard were particularly melancholy to behold, consisting mainly of 84XX and 94XX 0-6-0PTs which had completed very few years of service before withdrawal.

The Solution is Found

Except that the numbers of engines stored pending scrapping slowly increased, successive visits to Swindon at intervals of 2-3 months during 1958 and into 1959 showed little change in the contents of these dumps. By early 1959 the pressure on space for storage of withdrawn locomotives was becoming an acute problem at Swindon and at several other major works on other regions - Crewe, Derby, Horwich and the Glasgow area were also experiencing similar difficulties. A solution had to be found, and this was that the condemned engines would be sold to private firms for breaking up. For some time past the scrap metal dealers had been seeking new sources of steel scrap to meet the increasing demands of the post-war rebirth of the steel industry, and there were both financial and geographical factors acting in favour of their demands, as described in Chapter six. The replacement of some 16,000 locomotives and even larger numbers of other rolling stock was seen as a significant source of such scrap. A decision to release withdrawn engines was therefore welcomed by the scrap industry, whilst at the same time it could provide the railway operating regions with a solution to their problem of finding storage space for the condemned engines. To this decision, which was made by the early weeks of 1959, we owe the present phenomenon of Barry - which more than 50 years later exerts an ever-increasing fascination for its followers.

The sales begin

The condemned engines were sold at scrap prices, but there was also a charge based on the costs of transport and delivery to the purchasers premises. This was to be an important factor in determining which engines were purchased by particular contractors. As far as is known, the Western Region was first to commence sales of condemned engines, and the first purchasers were Messrs. Woodham Brothers of Barry Dock on 22 February 1959. The firm had long been in business at Barry, having interests in many aspects of the port's activities, of which the recovery and reclamation of metals from scrap was but one. Woodham Bros. had already developed an interest in the dismantling of surplus freight rolling stock and had established a base within the docks area at Barry for this purpose. It was a logical extension of this activity to purchase locomotives for dismantling, and with its ample siding accommodation and excellent facilities for shipping bulk materials Barry was a most suitable location from which to exploit the full potential of the

Above: A photograph showing the early days of wagon disposal at Barry. Woodhams used several tip lines which used to take coal to the hoist (shown on the right) where it was then tipped into a vessel. These wagons though were not going to be used for that purpose - they were being cut up and their steel and wood salvaged for scrap or re-use in the case of the timber. Thought to be number 26 Tip with the Rank Flour Mill in view. *Below:* One of the new road cranes purchased by Woodham Brothers. In the background is the yard used by the company for many of their operations. *Woodham family collection*

new opportunities.

Thus on 25 March 1959, the first batch of engines purchased by Woodham Bros. was despatched from Swindon Works yard as a special freight train to Barry Docks, departing from Swindon at 5.20 a.m. and arriving at Barry the same day. This method of delivery was to become the normal means of conveying condemned engines to their places of execution. On arrival at Barry, the locomotives were initially stored in the reception sidings serving No. 2 Dock, this being confirmed both by first-hand reports by local observers and by the address given in the Swindon sales records: 'Woodham Bros., No. 26 Tip, Barry Dock'. Since this first batch is of considerable historical interest, the identities of the engines concerned are worth recording: four Churchward 'Moguls', Nos. 5312, 5360/92/97. These were followed within a few days by the last survivor of the '3150' class, 2-6-2T No. 3170. These five engines had all spent several months on 'The Dump' at Swindon, and their final journey to Barry ensures them a small place in railway history.

Considering the tremendous growth of interest in Barry of recent years, the lack of information on the early years of locomotive dismantling there seems surprising. This is particularly true of Woodham Bros. initial purchases of 1959, even though they were important as almost certainly representing the first such transaction. Although all five locomotives were reported by various observers to have arrived at Barry, and their initial place of storage is also known, reports of the dates and site at which these engines were scrapped are extremely rare. From time to time there have been reports that a batch of locomotives was broken up in the locality of No.2 Dock, but no confirmation of dates or identities has been forthcoming and Woodham Bros. do not claim to have broken up any engines there. Of the initial batch, one at least (5312) was seen being towed through Barry Dock station, and was subsequently observed being cut up in a siding adjacent to Barry Works. This appears to confirm the fate for at least this particular engine, and the siding concerned (known locally as Luens Bank) was used by Woodhams for breaking up locomotives until at least mid-1961, this being confirmed by photographic evidence.

The initial purchases were followed after a few months by another batch of four Churchward 'Moguls', Nos. 5345/55, 6331/34, which were bought from Swindon in August 1959 and removed from 'The Dump' for movement to Barry. As with the previous batch, little is known about their later movements after arrival at Barry the following month.

More engines and more companies

After the commercial possibilities had been established by these transactions, Western Region and Woodham Bros. were soon to see sales of condemned engines increase considerably during the remainder of 1959. One of the more unlikely outcomes of these further sales was the purchase of veteran ex Midland Railway 0-6-0 tender engines by firms in the Glasgow area from the London Midland Region's dumps of withdrawn locomotives. The movement of these Derby built engines far from their usual haunts caused no little surprise at the time!

The next development at Barry was a most interesting one, for the company concerned was not Woodham Bros but another long-established Barry firm, Messrs J O Williams Ltd. This company's principal business was the importing and sale of timber and wood products, so when in September 1959 they entered the market as purchasers of condemned engines for scrap it was a considerable change of interest. The 12 engines bought by Williams consisted of small ex-GWR tank locomotives of the '14XX', '54XX', '57XX' and '74XX' classes and represented the first (and in some cases the only) examples of their types to be broken up at Barry. All 12 came from the Swindon Dump, leaving there in three batches each of four engines in late September 1959. After arrival at Barry, they were stored to await dismantling in the sidings which had been laid out on the infilled West Pond site. All 12 were observed there in mid-October 1959, but little is known about their subsequent fate or about the company that bought them. These 12 engines are notable for being the first to be dismantled on the West Pond site, which later became the scrapping area used by Woodham Bros. Undoubtedly partly responsible for the lack of information is the widespread but erroneous assumption that Woodham Bros. were the only contractors involved at Barry, whereas during research for this publication at least three other companies were identified.

During 1959 and 1960 whilst the numbers of engines sold remained relatively small, few locomotives survived long after arriving at Barry for breaking up. The 12 engines sold to J O Williams proved to be the only purchases made by that firm, though they were to remain in business at Barry until 1970. Thus Woodham Bros. once again resumed their leading role, but not yet on the scale that was soon to result in the creation of the familiar scenes of later years. In fact during 1960 the largest numbers of dumped engines at Barry were those stored in and around the running shed, though some of these were not at the time condemned and were later restored to service elsewhere. Of the engines that were purchased for scrap, 1960 was to bring the first examples of the relatively modern GWR classes of post-war vintage: the '41XX' 2-6-2 tanks and the '94XX' 0-6-0PT. Indeed, when purchased by Woodhams in November 1960 No.9499 of the latter class had seen barely four years of active service, an even shorter lifetime than that later achieved by certain of the BR class 9F 2-10-0s to be sent to Barry.

The Barry Legend is born

By early 1961, disposal of condemned engines to private contractors was a well established practice, increasing steadily as the rate of withdrawals and steam replacement programmes themselves increased. There was still little enthusiast interest in condemned engines, not surprisingly since there were still large numbers of locomotives in regular service. At Barry, however, 1961 saw the first examples of large-scale purchases, with nearly 40 locomotives being acquired by Woodhams between November 1960 and April 1961. Most of these purchases were broken up fairly soon after arrival, but some were to survive for several years and

As with many of the condemned locomotives, No. 30506 was towed dead to Barry. The convoy is seen at Gloucester in 1964. The engine hauling 30506 is a 'Grange' class which, had it stayed at Barry with the rest of the locomotives on arrival, might well have been saved for posterity. As it happens, the locomotive was not purchased by Woodhams and the class was made extinct. However, thanks to Barry scrapyard, a member of the Grange class is being re-constructed from other GWR engines saved from the yard. New-build *Betton Grange*, is being assembled at the Llangollen Railway.   *RH archives*

for one, GWR 'Small Prairie' No. 5552, the call to the breaker's torch never came at all! This engine was still in existence, though in a very dilapidated state, more than 20 years after its arrival at Barry - a unique link with the early years of this now famous scrapyard. This large build-up of engines early in 1961 resulted in many locomotives having to be stored whilst awaiting their turn to be broken up, and to accommodate them Woodhams arranged for the use of the low-level sidings adjacent to the West Pond site, where they were readily seen from the dock roads and from Barry Island. Thus from mid-1961 the first of what was to become a flood of visitors began to note the happenings at what was clearly no ordinary disposal yard.

Indeed, the events of early 1961 may truly be said to have laid the foundations of 'The Barry Legend', and to have earned for it the well-known and very descriptive title of 'The Graveyard of Steam'.

The engines came in two by two

Further purchases were made regularly for the next seven years, by which time the fame of Woodham Bros. yard had become known to enthusiasts far and near. A complete account of these years would be tedious for most readers, and all that will be attempted here is a brief summary of the more outstanding events.

1962

Most of the engines purchased by Woodhams were further examples of the various ex-GWR 'Prairie' tanks, but they were soon to be joined by more distinguished company in the shape of two 'King' class 4-6-0s. Except for their final years, these famous engines were relatively rare in South Wales, but a number saw out their time at Cardiff Canton shed until the last of the class was withdrawn in December 1962. Two of the engines condemned in June 1962 and which had then been sent to Swindon for disposal were destined to reach Barry under somewhat unusual circumstances, for when nos. 6023/4 were sold in October 1962 their purchasers were not Woodham Bros. but Messrs. T W Ward of Briton Ferry. When, however, the time came for the two locomotives to be moved from Swindon it was realised that 'King' class engines were not permitted to travel over the South Wales main line beyond Cardiff, which they would have to do to reach Messrs. Wards' yard. The sale was accordingly cancelled until a solution could be found, and the two locomotives were both still at Swindon in mid-November.

After special agreement had been given to their movement over the short distance from Cardiff to Barry, Woodham Bros. were allowed to purchase them late in November. Nos. 6023/4 arrived at Barry early in 1963 and subsequently attracted much attention during their long stays at Barry.

1963

The range of classes represented increased with the acquisition of examples of the '28XX' Churchward 2-8-0s, and more named locomotives including 'Castle' and 'Hall' class 4-6-0s were purchased. Locomotives were now being broken up on the West Pond site. Over 50 engines remained to be dealt with at the year end. An interesting development was the purchase of a batch of War Dept. 0-6-0STs which arrived by road transport rather than by rail.

1964

Because of the continuing increase in the numbers of purchases, a second dump was established in the sidings on the higher level near to Barry Works, engines being first noted there in January. Until now, all ex-BR locomotives purchased by Woodhams had been of ex-GWR origin, but from mid-1964 engines from other regions began to appear. These included Southern Region 'S15' 4-6-0s and Maunsell 2-6-0s, whilst the first deliveries of Bulleid Pacifics began in November. Another arrival destined for subsequent fame was 45690 *Leander* together with the two ex-S&D 2-8-0s, all these latter engines being withdrawn from sheds then under Western Region control. The year end total of over 110 locomotives was more than double that for 12 months previously.

1965

Two more companies joined the ranks of the Barry disposal contractors: Messrs. Woodfields Ltd. who operated from Cadoxton Goods Yard for a brief period before moving to larger premises at Newport, and Messrs. R S Tyley Ltd. who were engaged on the track-lifting contract on the former Barry Railway line from

Cadoxton to Treforest, and used locomotives of the '42XX', '16XX' and '94XX' classes which they subsequently scrapped at both Barry and Cadoxton. Meanwhile at Woodhams the early months of 1965 saw more than 30 locomotives scrapped, but many more were still being purchased including more Bulleid Pacifics, another 'Jubilee' (45699 *Galatea*) and several Stanier 2-8-0s. Towards the end of 1965 considerable numbers of BR Standard locomotives began to appear, especially the 4MT 2-6-4T and 9F 2-10-0 designs. A batch of Stanier 'Black Five' 4-6-0s became the most distant acquisitions to reach Barry after being purchased from as far away as Carlisle! This demonstrated the rapid rate of steam replacement from local areas, but by October 1965 Woodham Bros. had ceased scrapping on a large scale. By the year end some 150 engines were dumped in the Barry area, but many more were on the way.

1966-1970
From 1966 onwards the increase in numbers proceeded steadily as will be seen from the following figures:

January 1966:	154
January 1967:	177
January 1968:	209
February 1969:	218 (removals for preservation commenced September 1968)

The maximum appears to have been about 221 locomotives in mid-1968.

One of the 213 locomotive's to depart from Barry following a stay of execution from Woodham's yard. No. 6023 *King Edward II* was the 159th engine to depart from Barry, which it did in December 1984 destined for a siding next to Temple Meads station in Bristol. It was subsequently purchased by the Great Western Society at Didcot.

Notable arrivals during this period included the solitary BR Class 8P 4-6-2 No. 71000 *Duke of Gloucester*, and the only engine of ex-LNER design ever to reach Barry, Thompson 'B1' 4-6-0 No. 61264 which arrived in June 1968 after serving as a stationary boiler at Colwick. Since by then the Nottingham area was under the control of the London Midland Region, no steam locomotive from the E.R. was ever to arrive at Woodhams. Sales of condemned engines from the Western and Southern Regions ended in 1966 and 1967 respectively, and for their final purchases of steam locomotives Woodham Bros. returned to the LMR by purchasing engines from as far afield as Northwich, Patricroft and Carnforth. Together with other locos from the Lancashire area, these arrived at Barry in September 1968, by which time purchases for preservation had commenced with the sale of Fowler '4F' No. 43924 to the Keighley & Worth Valley Railway.

Very few diesel locomotives were bought by Woodhams, but two of the NBL 'Warship' class diesel-hydraulics (D600/1) arrived in November 1968 together with one of their smaller sisters by the same builder (D6122). Last of all the purchases was D8206, ironically enough from the Eastern Region, which was bought in April 1969.

During most of this period no locomotives were cut up, though 1970 saw the demise of D600 and D8206. The 'Barry Legend' was now gathering momentum, and during the next few years it was to become increasingly important due to the upsurge of interest in railway preservation, which found in Barry a focus for its efforts.

1970s, the peak period for departures

If the 1960s were the years of purchases at Barry, then the 1970s were surely the years of sales. After the slow but sure beginnings in 1968-69, the numbers of engines purchased by preservationists increased steadily to proportions almost as impressive as the build-up in those of purchases some years previously. The annual totals of engines sold are shown below:

Locomotives departing from Barry

Before	1970:	3	1972:	10	1975:	14	1978:	11
	1970:	8	1973:	18	1976:	8	1979:	11
	1971:	6	1974:	19	1977:	1		

Analysis of these purchases shows some interesting features. At the start of the period, funds for purchase were usually raised by the announcement of schemes to save engines of special interest, and in this way examples of most of the classes represented at Barry had been purchased by the mid-1970s. Attention was rightly concentrated on types with single representatives at Barry, followed by the better examples of classes with several examples, and other locomotives particularly suited to the requirements of operating preserved railways. After about 1975, however, would-be purchasers could no longer find suitable candidates which satisfied all these criteria, and by 1977 it appeared that the 'Barry Boom Years' were finally over. Such was the growth of interest in and support for railway preservation, however, that in the later 1970s a renewal of activity and purchasing took place, and many more locomotives were bought. These came almost entirely from classes from which examples had already been saved, and inevitably resulted in considerable duplication. This proliferation of schemes to preserve particular engines, which were not in all cases entirely justifiable on the merits of the locomotives concerned or their usefulness for future operation, was to give rise to considerable comment and criticism.

In addition to the purchases made by individual owners, there was also a marked growth in acquisitions by, or on behalf of, established steam railways who had realised the need to safeguard their future motive power requirements. Restoration of suitable engines from Barry was seen as the best method of ensuring continuity of operation with steam traction. And as steadily as the numbers of locomotives remaining at Barry decreased, interest in them grew - and in doing so gave rise to considerable debate within the preservation movement. A temporary slackening in the availability of wagon contracts led to a resumption of locomotive dismantling by Woodhams in the summer of 1980 and this provided a stimulus to further purchases.

As Barry and its dwindling number of engines entered the 1980s, the need for a more united voice about their future became increasingly apparent. As an important first step, an Action Group was formed with the specific purpose of drawing attention to the Barry engines, and this later developed into an organisation capable of rendering 'first aid' to engines worthy of preservation. Valuable assistance was also forthcoming from other sources, particularly the Association of Railway Preservation Societies. The efforts of the late Robert Adley MP succeeded in placing the issues before Parliament, and were instrumental in the formulation of the 'Barry Rescue Project' which was launched early in 1981 and brought together all these various individual organisations with the active co-operation of the National Railway Museum authorities. All relevant viewpoints were represented when questions concerning the future of the engines still left at Barry were concerned.

The urgency of these efforts had been stimulated by the realisation that time would eventually run out for the locomotives still un-purchased.

Ex-BR locomotive engineer's, John Peck and George Knight, were called in by 'Barry Rescue' to inspect the remaining locomotives in the yard during 1981. They found that all the engine's could be saved and restored given the appropriate funding.

Chapter Six
SCRAP, STEEL AND STEAM ENGINES

No account of the eventful railway history of Barry would be complete without an attempt to explain the survival of some 200 locomotives for so long after their disposal by British Railways. When the first edition of this book was written there were two main theories :

1.   That Woodham Bros. foresaw the growth of interest in railway preservation, and retained their locomotives for resale.

2.   That the locomotives were purchased for export as scrap, but this proved impracticable and no other outlet for them could be found.

We now know that neither of those possibilities was correct. All of the contractors involved in the purchase and dismantling of condemned locomotives did so for the conventional commercial motives of profit, and Woodham bros. were no exception to this rule.

A Problem of Space - and Sales Potential

Returning briefly to the origins of the decision in 1959, it will be remembered that the principal problem faced by the railway authorities was that of finding sufficient storage accommodation for the increasing numbers of withdrawn engines. Whilst this was probably the most important factor that contributed to the decision, it was undoubtedly not the only one, for there was another and very significant trend in progress at the time when the BR Modernisation Plan was beginning to show its earliest results. This was the growth in demand for steel scrap, a commodity for which demand for both home and overseas markets was increasing steadily in the late 1950s.

The scrap metal industry was eager to take full advantage of the favourable commercial opportunities, while in contrast it was relatively difficult for the nationalised British Railways system to exploit these markets, except indirectly via the private sector of the scrap metal industry. The railways were traditionally an important source of scrap metals for which no further internal use could be found: materials such as worn-out rails, wheels, axles and other components were commonly re-sold to their original makers, to be recovered in the form of new production. From about 1957 onwards these limited quantities were augmented by the release of complete wagons surplus to BR requirements under the Modernisation Programme, and many contractors including Woodham Bros. purchased such wagons for dismantling. The demand was, however, such that still greater quantities of scrap steel were needed, and during 1958 the possibility of making additional supplies available was discussed between the railway authorities and the representatives of the scrap metal industry. As we have already seen, these discussions, together with the growing problem of storage space for condemned engines, eventually led to the decision to sell complete locomotives to private contractors by the early months of 1959. Two important principles had thus been established: firstly, the demand, and secondly the supply. A third and equally important principle was that of location, which in the case of Barry - and indeed of South Wales in general - was particularly significant.

Meanwhile the position concerning the export of scrap metals was changing dramatically. Although it was not unknown for surplus scrap to be exported when domestic demand was low, the quantities involved were quite small and subject to control by legislation intended to ensure a reliable supply for the home market. After 1957, however, a change in the controls produced the trend shown by the following table:

Exports of iron and steel scrap and waste

	1956	1957	1958	1959	1960
Quantities in thousands of tons	6.0	3.1	242.8	933.1	17.9

(Source: Iron & Steel Statistics Bureau)

The remarkable increase from 1957 to 1959 led to a re-imposition of the controls for 1960 and 1961, but thereafter further changes produced even greater quantities being exported with amounts in excess of one million tons being recorded in 1962, 1963 and 1967. While the greater proportion of the exported scrap was destined for European steelworks, significant quantities for destinations as far away as India and Japan were involved with certain consignments being shipped from Barry Docks to these countries during the 1960s.

The steel industry in South Wales

In South Wales the steel-making industry originated with the early ironworks of the Aberdare, Merthyr and Tredegar areas and the tinplate works of the Llanelly and Swansea districts. Increasing dependence on imported iron ore after the local supplies had been exhausted led to a move towards the ports; this geographical shift being favoured by the topographical nature of the region, which did not favour inland sites that would need expensive haulage of bulk materials uphill away from the coast. Thus later steelworks became established at such sites as Ebbw Vale (an exception to the preference for coastal sites), Cardiff, Port Talbot, Briton Ferry and Llanelly, and there was a gradual reduction in the numbers of small tinplate works.

A 16-ton mineral wagon is being cut up by one of Woodham's employees in August 1979. Thousands of items of rolling stock would be dismantled on this site from the mid 1950s. *M J Beckett*

By the 1950s South Wales was the leading steel-making district in Britain, and in 1960 its ingot production was some 16% greater than that of the next largest producer, North East England. Because of the scrap demand represented by the long-established local tinplate industry, South Wales had traditionally relied on a greater proportion of 'imported' scrap than had other districts. In addition, lacking the large centres of population and heavy engineering industries which are the usual sources of scrap arising for steel-making, the region became increasingly deficient in locally available supplies of scrap. For these reasons a price differential had developed and scrap prices in South Wales were among the highest in Britain: the following examples of prices current in early 1963 will serve to illustrate this point.

Region	Price (s.d. per ton)
Midlands	220s 0d
Sheffield	226s 3d
N E England	228s 3d
South Wales (East)	227s 3d
South Wales (West)	232s 3d
Scotland	229s 3d

Although there were temporary fluctuations in the demand for scrap, the trend throughout the 1950s was one of steady growth. In South Wales this trend was particularly exemplified by the construction of a major new integrated steel works at Llanwern near Newport, and by the substantial modernisation and enlargement of the existing plant at Port Talbot.

With all these factors operating together it will readily be appreciated why when sales of condemned locomotives began in 1959, contractors in South Wales were not slow to see the commercial opportunities. The subsequent sale of such large numbers of engines to firms in this region confirms how successfully the contractors identified and met the demand.

Barry takes the lead

Once the decision to release condemned engines for dismantling by private contractors had been taken, companies in the Barry area were among the first to take advantage. Both Woodham Bros. and J O Williams Ltd purchased batches of engines from Swindon during 1959, as described in the previous chapter. Although not located in the immediate vicinity of any of the South Wales steel plants (that at East Moors, Cardiff being the nearest), Barry had good rail communications with the other centres, with the additional advantage of its spacious port layout with ample land available for industrial development close to the docks. Infilling of the former West Pond in the years immediately after 1945 had still further increased the area of available land, and this site was to prove particularly valuable when the numbers of engines stored at Barry awaiting dismantling increased after 1961.

At first, however, condemned engines arriving at Barry were broken up very rapidly. This supports the view that the contractors were operating according to principles which would assure them of a rapid return for their investments. All locomotives purchased during 1959 and 1960 were soon broken up, and the early months of 1961 showed that the emphasis at that time was still on dismantling. Some 40% of all the engines broken up at Barry since purchases commenced were broken up in these first three years. Comparatively smaller numbers of locomotives were broken up by Woodhams between 1962 and 1964, but by this time several other contractors elsewhere in South Wales had entered the market. The first nine months of 1965 saw another peak of dismantling activity at Barry, with another 50 locomotives being scrapped by Woodham Bros. The principal activity at Woodhams since 1965 has been that of breaking up rolling stock rather than locomotives. Although by weight a steam locomotive consists principally of steel and other ferrous metal such as castings, a considerable part of its value as scrap may in fact be represented by non-ferrous components, such as copper in fireboxes, pipework and fittings, brasswork items, bearings etc. However, to dismantle a locomotive in such a way as to separate out these more valuable components without loss or damage requires much greater care and effort on the part of the scrap dealer: the work must proceed slowly and carefully if the maximum value is to be realised. In contrast, vehicles consisting mainly of sheet metal on steel under-frames can be rapidly broken up with relatively little difficulty. It is perhaps worthy of note that Dai Woodham referred to the difficulty of dealing with the fireboxes of dismantled engines, which at one time caused the firm to seriously consider withdrawing from the market as purchasers of condemned locomotives. It was, therefore, quite logical for the engines to be retained intact in order to concentrate on the rolling stock contracts, which were to continue well into the 1980s. By doing so, the company was able to protect the investment represented by the more valuable components in the locomotives and ensure continuity of employment for the workforce.

Barry has also long been active as a port from which significant quantities of

A copper firebox is extracted from the frames of a locomotive being dismantled in 1959 at the yard of Woodham Brothers. The company at first sent this whole section to an engineering company in Barry docks for stripping out the copper from the steel, but this practise was stopped after a short period.

scrap metals were exported. This activity was certainly practised within a few years of the commencement of locomotive disposals at Barry, and in 1963 for example it was reported that a total of some 82,000 tons of steel scrap was sent overseas from Barry by four companies. The principal destinations of such consignments were at first limited to European countries, particularly Spain, but by 1967 shipments were being made to purchasers in Asia.

When the first edition of this book was being prepared in the early 1980s, around 150 locomotives had been purchased from the Barry yard, leaving at least another 60 still with their futures to be resolved.

Proposals for saving these final occupants now came under the remit of the 'Barry Steam Locomotive Action Group' (BSLAG) led by Francis Blake, with the aim of co-ordinating negotiations between Woodham Brothers and the various parties interested in purchasing the engines. The remaining locomotives were professionally examined by experienced former BR locomotive engineers. It was found that every engine was potentially capable of restoration, though the process would be time-consuming, expensive and demanding.

With the involvement in 1980-82 of the late Robert Adley MP an organisation known as 'Barry Rescue' was formed with the objective of saving the engines still surviving at Barry.

Progress was slow but steady but as the end of the 1980s approached another factor became relevant, namely that Dai Woodham was approaching the age of 70 and would like to retire and close the yard at that time. This raised fears that that the remaining engines still left in the yard could be broken up before they could be saved.

Ten of the locomotives were passed into the ownership of South Glamorgan County Council with the intention that they would be kept together as a collection which would form the basis of a Welsh Railway Museum to be established in the former Bute Docks area at Cardiff.

These ten locomotives were actually moved to Cardiff but the proposed museum project did not materialise because the area was chosen as a base for the new Welsh Assembly and other 'Cardiff Bay' projects. The engines were eventually taken back to Barry for storage under the auspices of the Vale of Glamorgan District Council with a view to become part of the new line being formed at Barry with headquarters at Barry Island Station.

The Barry Island Railway operated for a few years but has changed hands at the time of writing with some of the 'Barry 10' going to other preservation projects around Britain - see 'The Barry List' section within this book.

Thus it can be seen that the far-reaching decision in 1965 made by Woodham Brothers to concentrate on breaking up rolling stock rather than locomotives will have important effects for the railway preservation movement far into the future.

When Dai Woodham first became involved with the breaking up of redundant BR wagons in 1957, not even he could have forseen the consequences of that decision. The extensive and continued development of railway preservation in Britain 50 years afterwards, is a fitting tribute to a remarkable man.

Above: No. 4164 waits for the men and cranes to start breaking up its Swindon-built structure. The engine had arrived in May 1960. No. 4164 steamed into the yard as the connecting rods were still in place and its cabside and smokebox number plates also in situ, see back cover. *Below:* An early crane used by Woodham's being assembled for use. *Woodham family collection*

Locomotives scrapped at Barry

Loco	Date withdrawn	Last shed	Date sold	Cut up by *	Notes
1367	10 1964	Wadebridge	11 1964	2 1965	
1368	10 1964	Wadebridge	11 1964	2 1965	
1428	6 1959	Gloucester	9 1959	6 1960	Sold to J O William
1457	3 1959	Oswestry	9 1959	6 1960	Sold to J O William
1639	11 1964	Worcester	1 1965	4 1965	R S Tyley (Note 1)
3170	8 1958	Ebbw Jct	2 1959	9 1959	Last of 3150 class
3727	4 1964	Barry	6 1964	1 1965	
3794	12 1964	Oxford	2 1965	8 1965	
3817	8 1965	Croes Newydd	10 1965	3 1973	
4156	6 1965	Severn Tunnel Jct	7 1965	7 1980	
4157	6 1965	Severn Tunnel Jct	7 1965	9 1965	
4164	1 1960	Severn Tunnel Jct	5 1960	12 1960	
4283	10 1964	Barry	11 1964	3 1965	R S Tyley (Note 2)
4295	12 1964	Pontypool Rd	2 1965	3 1965	R S Tyley (Note 3)
4550	10 1960	Neyland	3 1961	6 1961	
4559	10 1960	St Blazey	3 1961	6 1961	
4594	11 1960	Neyland	3 1961	6 1961	
5182	5 1962	Gloucester	8 1962	7 1964	
5312	10 1958	Oxley	2 1959	8 1959	
5345	6 1959	Pontypool Rd	8 1959	10 1959	
5355	4 1959	Kidderminster	8 1959	10 1959	
5360	9 1958	Cardiff Canton	2 1959	8 1959	
5392	8 1958	Worcester	2 1959	8 1959	
5397	7 1958	Didcot	2 1959	8 1959	
5407	6 1960	Banbury	11 1960	8 1961	
5417	1 1961	Banbury	4 1961	6 1961	
5422	6 1960	Oswestry	11 1960	2 1965	
5423	6 1959	Westbury	9 1959	6 1960	Sold to J O William
5424	4 1959	Banbury	9 1959	6 1960	Sold to J O William
5504	10 1960	Taunton	1 1961	6 1961	
5510	10 1960	Machynlleth	3 1961	4 1965	
5514	11 1960	Gloucester	3 1961	6 1961	
5546	9 1960	Neyland	1 1961	6 1961	
5547	2 1962	Swindon	5 1962	3 1965	
5557	10 1960	St Blazey	1 1961	8 1965	
5558	10 1960	Newton Abbot	1 1961	8 1965	
5651	12 1964	Rhymney	2 1965	5 1965	
5669	9 1964	Radyr	11 1964	2 1965	Note 4
5707	3 1959	Tondu	9 1959	6 1960	Sold to J O William
5734	5 1959	Newport Pill	9 1959	6 1960	Sold to J O William
5794	12 1959	Aberbeeg	1 1961	8 1965	
6115	11 1964	Severn Tnl Jct	1 1965	4 1965	
6131	9 1964	Reading	10 1964	2 1965	Scrapped Woodfield

Loco	Date withdrawn	Last shed	Date sold	Cut up by*	Notes
6331	4 1959	Banbury	8 1959	10 1959	
6334	4 1959	Swindon	8 1959	10 1959	
6406	6 1960	Laira	11 1960	6 1961	
6621	12 1964	Radyr	2 1965	3 1965	
6696	12 1963	Barry	2 1964	4 1964	
6711	6 1959	Newport Pill	9 1959	6 1960	Sold to J O Williams
6736	2 1959	Swindon	9 1959	6 1960	Sold to J O Williams
6743	4 1959	Newport Pill	9 1959	6 1960	Sold to J O Williams
6753	1 1961	Swansea E. Dock	4 1961	6 1961	
6945	9 1964	Cardiff E. Dock	10 1964	2 1965	Scrapped Woodfields
7226	11 1964	Aberdare	1 1965	3 1965	
7411	5 1959	Oxford	9 1959	6 1960	Sold to J O Williams
7447	4 1959	Stourbridge Jct	9 1959	6 1960	Sold to J O Williams
7702	9 1960	Leamington	1 1961	6 1961	
7712	7 1960	Pontypool Rd	11 1960	6 1961	
7722	10 1960	Stourbridge Jct	1 1961	8 1965	
7723	8 1960	Gloucester LMR	11 1960	2 1965	

Churchward 2-6-0 No. 5392 was the first ever locomotive cut up by Woodhams. It was dismantled during 1959. The engine arrived in the March with 5312, 5360 and 5397, the first group of engines sold by Swindon Works to a private contractor. It is viewed just prior to cutting up starting at the power house site at Barry. *Woodham family collection*

Loco	Date withdrawn	Last shed	Date sold	Cut up by*	Notes
7725	8 1960	Tondu	11 1960	6 1961	
7735	5 1959	Tyseley	9 1959	6 1960	Sold to J O William
7758	6 1960	Duffryn Yard	11 1960	2 1962	
8419	1 1960	Barry	3 1961	5 1965	
8473	1 1961	Penzance	3 1961	8 1961	
8475	9 1964	Radyr	11 1964	1 1965	Note 4
8479	10 1964	Radyr	11 1964	3 1965	
8749	10 1964	Gloucester	11 1964	2 1965	
9436	7 1960	Landore	11 1960	6 1961	
9438	6 1959	Gloucester	11 1960	6 1961	
9439	6 1959	Exeter	11 1960	6 1961	
9443	6 1959	Cardiff Canton	11 1960	6 1961	
9445	1 1960	Gloucester	1 1961	1 1965	
9449	6 1960	Banbury	1 1961	1 1965	
9459	9 1959	Aberbeeg	11 1960	6 1961	
9462	11 1960	Newton Abbot	3 1961	5 1965	
9468	8 1960	Ebbw Jct	1 1961	8 1965	
9488	4 1965	Radyr	4 1965	9 1965	R S Tyley (Note 5)
9491	6 1959	Swansea E.Dock	11 1960	3 1965	
9492	6 1959	Gloucester	11 1960	2 1962	
9496	12 1959	Stafford Rd	11 1960	6 1961	
9499	9 1959	St Philips Marsh	11 1960	3 1965	
30512	3 1964	Feltham	12 1964	1 1965	
30844	6 1964	Feltham	12 1964	1 1965	
34045	6 1964	Bournemouth	2 1965	3 1965	
34094	8 1964	Nine Elms	12 1964	1 1965	
41248	11 1964	Barnstaple	2 1965	3 1965	
41303	10 1964	Bournemouth	2 1965	3 1965	
76080	12 1967	Springs Branch	1 1968	4 1972	
80067	6 1965	Bristol Barrow Rd	8 1965	9 1965	
92085	12 1966	Birkenhead	5 1967	7 1980	
92232	12 1964	Cardiff East Dock		3 1965	
D600	12 1967	Laira	7 1968	1970	
D601	12 1967	Laira	7 1968	7 1980	
D6122	12 1967	Hither Green	6 1968	6 1980	
D8206	9 1968	Stratford	4 1969	1970	

War Dept 0-6-0ST

Loco	Date withdrawn	Last shed	Date sold	Cut up by*	Notes
WD 106	12 1961	Marchwood	7 1963	3 1965	Built Hunslet 1943
WD 108		Longmoor	8 1963	3 1965	Built Hunslet 1943
WD 119			1963	3 1965	Built Barclay 1944
WD 130			1963	3 1965	Built Hunslet 1944
WD 178	1958	Longmoor	8 1963	3 1965	Built R.S&H 1945
WD 203	7 1963	Longmoor	7 1963	3 1965	Built Hunslet 1953

Locomotives broken up at Barry Works by BR

37	9 1956	10 1956	Rhymney Rly 0-6-2T	
296	9 1949	1950	Taff Vale Rly 0-6-2T	
1141	7 1952	1952	Swansea Harbour Trust	
1461	5 1958	9 1958		
5792	10 1956	11 1956		

* Locomotive cut up by the last day of month shown. Dates for 1959-60 are less certain.

Summary of locomotives broken up in the Barry area:

Woodham Brothers, Barry Dock, (1959-80)	: 84
J O Williams Ltd., Barry Dock (1959)	: 1
I C Woodfield, Cadoxton (1964-65)	: 2
R S Tyley Ltd., Barry and Cadoxton (1965)	: 4
BR Barry Works (1950-58)	: 5
Total locomotives scrapped at Barry	**: 107**

1. Sold to Steel Supply Co. (Western) Ltd., Briton Ferry, January 1965. Re-sold or hired to R S Tyley Ltd. for use on track-lifting work on former Barry Railway main line from Cadoxton to Tonteg Jct as from 1st February 1965, but out of use by mid-April 1965 and scrapped near Barry Works later that Month.

2. Sold to Steel Supply Co. (Western) Ltd., Jersey Marine, November 1964. Re-sold or hired to RS Tyley Ltd. for use on track-lifting contract (see 1639) but found unsuitable and subsequently broken up near Barry Works in late March 1965.

3. Sold to Cox & Danks Ltd., February 1965 and intended for use by R S Tyley Ltd. on track-lifting contract (see 1639), but unlikely to have actually been used. Scrapped near Barry Works in late March 1965 together with 4283.

4. Both engines originally sold to Woodfields, Cadoxton in October 1964. Re-sold in November 1964 to Woodham Bros., Barry Dock, and subsequently scrapped there.

5. Sold to Steel Supply Co. (Western) Ltd., April 1965, and consigned to R S Tyley Ltd. for use on Barry Railway track-lifting contract, where it replaced 1639. Used until completion of contract and subsequently scrapped at Cadoxton in September 1965.

A general view of Woodhams' first locomotive cutting up area near the power house. All manner of scrap material was sorted here after either a wagon or engine was scrapped. The Barry Works buildings are still visible in the background. They were all demolished after 1965.

The Barry List

Tenth Edition

Information correct to 1st August 2010

Compiled by
Roger Hardingham

Introduction

This tenth and most likely last, edition of The Barry List, brings the story of the locomotives hauled out of the yard at Woodham Brothers up to date as at 1st August 2010. Clearly the number purchased and moved from Barry has remained unchanged at 213 locomotives, but the story of those now sited around the various preserved railways in Britain is an ever-changing one.

At the present time, 138 locomotives out of the 213 preserved have now steamed once more following restoration from Barry condition - a remarkable achievement by all concerned. There are to be several more being brought back to life and will appear over the coming months bringing a total of more than 150 operational engines ever more likely. Calculations show that nine locomotives listed in the following pages will never steam again. These are made up from engines such as *Ellerman Lines* which was sectioned for display at the National Railway Museum, but also others such as *Maindy Hall* which is being canabalised to recreate a long-lost type, in this case a GWR Saint Class. That leaves 66 locomotives around the UK that require restoration, a little over a third of the original number removed from the yard.

It is now 20 years since the final departure of a locomotive from the yard. No. 5553 left Barry in January 1990 for restoration to working order. After the failure of the Bute Road project within the Cardiff Bay area, 10 Barry engines actually returned to several off-line locations in Barry before going into storage in the ex-wagon repair shed close to Barry Town station. A new scheme was launched in May 2010 to bring new life to these locomotives, with two remaining at Barry.

More than 50 years have passed since this phenomenon started at Barry and the town and port has changed dramatically since the late 1950s. This whole saga has also transformed the preservation map of Britain and has seen a multi-million pound industry develop from the simple business of a scrap merchant in the town of Barry in South Wales.

The Woodham Family Archive

Meeting with the Woodham family and delving into their archives has revealed some interesting facts about the family business. The more recent businesses set up after World War Two were developed from the scrap and recycling of items from the port of Barry and the many ships based there. Hundreds of different parts from the shipping trade were to be bought and sold after deals were stuck with the ship's owners. Rope was to be a major item recycled in the early years and photographs are available of lorry loads being taken away.

The five Woodham brothers would at some point become involved in the businesses but it would be David Lloyd Victor Woodham (Dai) that would stand out as being the one most capable of taking the family firm forward and into prosperity. Dai was a genius when it came to dealing with people across the whole spectrum of life and it was his business acumen and shrewd judgment that made the many different business prosper.

One other brother did work alongside Dai very well until his untimely death. Billy Woodham was engaged in the business when the locomotives started to swell the yards in Barry docks and Dai admitted that he (Billy) was a driving force in persuading him to retain the locomotives rather than scrap them during the hectic years of wagon contracts and locomotive purchases. When the period in question is analysed, you can almost see the commercial dilemmas being considered by Woodhams in the 1950s and 60s.

The modernisation of British Railways and indeed of Britain as a whole, was producing millions and millions of tons of scrap metal of all types. It wasn't just locomotives and wagons, it would be ships, both naval and merchant and aircraft and many other assets from government and industry.

Dai Woodham arrives at his site in the West Pond area by his famous mode of transport - a Rolls Royce. His business acumen had earned his success in the scrap trade within Barry.

Without knowledge of the inner business details of Woodhams, you have to consider the effect of rapid growth in their businesses at this time. Like any firm, cash flow could well have affected bidding for disposals at certain times which might explain why some BR wagon or locomotive purchases have gaps in them and the contract let to another metal merchant. Clearly the old redundant sidings in the Barry dock area were full of wagons ready to meet their end and this too would probably answer why the purchasing of condemned rolling stock was inconsistent - there probably was no room to accommodate them. As we know locomotives also started to build up in the old tip sidings (top yards) and then the West Pond site (bottom yard) which were also sidings once used for the coal export trade.

A redundant 'tip' line in No. 2 Dock used for the breaking of wagons. The axles of some scrapped wagons and locomotives were exported to France for high-quality steel wire production. This photograph gives a remarkable insight to the detail of the coal tipping hoist arrangement. The Rank Flour Mill is in the background. *Woodham family collection*

BR Modernisation Plan saves steam!

In a strange twist of fate, it was the very fact that BR was modernising its network that in the end saved so many steam locomotives for us to enjoy today. Had it not been for the vast amounts of rolling stock such as wagons and carriages coming up for disposal at the crucial periods between the 1960s and the 1980s, the incredible total of 213 engines preserved around the country from this one source would simply not have happened. We know that these locomotives were only spared the torch because Woodhams had so much else to cut up.

The South Wales steel connection

The steelworks at Margam, originally and colloquially known as the 'Abbey Works', correctly termed today as 'Corus Strip Products UK Port Talbot Works', began production in 1953. Several steel manufacturers in South Wales pooled their resources to form 'The Steel Company of Wales' and construct a modern integrated steelworks on a site then owned by Guest, Keen and Baldwins. At the time of peak employment in the 1960s, the Abbey Works was Europe's largest steelworks and the largest single employer in Wales, with a labour force of 18,000.

The position of the works at Margam and the new plant at Llanwern near Newport, formerly the Spencer Works, which opened in 1962, created a huge demand for the supply of raw materials. Ralph Brett worked at the BR Divisional Manager's office in Cardiff and became the liaison contact between Dai Woodham and the Derby Supplies Office. He recalls arranging for the inspection of condemned stock based on the BRB's condemnation programme. "Dai told me once in the early 1960s that with the new steel works in South Wales and the BRB's intention of disposing of thousands of redundant wagons, that he (Dai) was going to get on that 'gravy train'. "Ralph says that "Woodham's were well placed at Barry for the breaking up contracts due to the large numbers of redundant sidings available within the old port area, and therefore the space to store and cut up rolling stock." He would also be, "very good at returning some re-useable components back to BR if required, such as axle boxes and bearings."

The effect of Woodhams yard on preservation in Britain

There is no doubt that railway preservation in the UK today would be very limited had the introduction of 213 locomotives into the fleets of preserved railways not occurred. A survey of the top 16 preserved railway sites in Britain show that out of 262 ex BR standard gauge locomotives in their stock lists, 162 come from Barry. Railways such as the Mid-Hants, West Somerset, Llangollen Swanage and Torbay steam railways rely totally on ex Barry engines. To a lesser, but still to a crucial level, others in the table below also rely on restored engines from Woodham's yard.

The only railways which could have probably survived without this influx of motive power include the Bluebell, North York Moors, South Devon and possibly others. However, the 'strain' put on the fleet of locomotives bought from BR direct would have quite likely jeopardised the operation of any railway solely relying on that small number of engines. Certainly, expansion of running lengths and services at some railways would simply not have happened.

The multi-million pound businesses made up of preserved railways turnover, economic impact in local surrounding areas, the repairing services, publishing of magazines, main line steam and photography businesses set up after the 'Barry boom' would not be around or be anywhere near as successful had it not been for Woodhams. Annual turnover in all these areas approaches £100 million.

A Survey of Preserved Railway Sites with Ex-British Railways Locomotives

Name	Barry Locos	Non Barry Locos	Total
Bluebell Railway	11	17	28
Bodmin Railway	3	3	6
East Lancs Railway	11	5	16
Great Central Railway	7	5	12
Great Western Society	11	8	19
Keighley & Worth Valley	6	11	17
Llangollen Railway	11	3	14
Mid-Hants Railway	16	2	18
Midland Railway	8	4	12
North York Moors Railway	9	12	21
Severn Valley Railway	15	11	26
South Devon Railway	3	5	8
Swanage Railway	8	1	9
Torbay Railway	6	-	6
Birmingham Railway Centre	10	5	15
West Somerset Railway	14	-	14
Totals	**162**	**100**	**262**

As can be seen, the Mid-Hants Railway currently has the largest fleet of ex Barry engines in Britain followed closely by the Severn Valley and West Somerset railways. Many are totally reliant on Barry locomotives. The 'missing' engines (51 in number) are made up of numerous engines scattered around the UK at various other railway sites and even airfields and farms! When looking at the 66 locomotives still to steam, you wonder whether all of them will ever do so. Will every Merchant Navy Pacific for example make it to the running line again, there are still six potentials. Or will we ever see other classes which have large numbers still in ex Barry condition. We will have to wait and see, but the crucial point is that they *are* still around and are either possibilities for restoration or for use in giving up vital spare parts one day to another engine. The heroic actions of the Barry Steam Locomotive Action Group of the early 1980s had that vision and thank goodness they did.

Locomotives arrive at Barry

As we have seen in the first section of this book, engines started to arrive at Barry in March 1959 after Woodham Brothers bid for the first series of engines that Swindon Works put out to private buyers. From then onwards a steady stream of locomotives were bought, including 12 purchased later in 1959 by the other company at Barry, J O Williams Ltd, who cut up their one-off purchases quite quickly. Both Woodham Brothers and J O Williams were cutting up wagons too, with the former starting this during 1957 at the redundant coal tip sidings north of No. 1 Dock.

As the first two or three years passed by, all engines that arrived at Barry were subsequently cut up. The longest serving resident was No. 5552 which arrived in 1960 and lasted in the yard right up until 1986 - after 26 years at Barry! This situation was simply due to the location of the engine within the various storage lines and whether it was shunted around the yard which put it at the rear of another group of locomotives and out of reach of the men cutting up. These circumstances played a large part in the reasons for later engines being cut up. No. 3817 and 76080 were broken up because they were the first in the line and nearest to the cutting up areas. In the case of 3817 it was noted in 1968 near the back of scrap line number seven. However, 4F No. 43924 was behind it and so when this first locomotive to leave the yard was ready to go it had to be shunted out for its transport to West Yorkshire. This change in order revealed No. 3817 to the 'danger' area of the cutting lines and was subsequently cut up in 1973. As for No. 76080, it was one of the last steam locomotives to arrive at Barry and was probably shunted on to the end of a line and close at hand.

The situation of shear bad luck in location within the sidings would occur again in July 1980 to Nos. 4156 and 92085 which happened to be the closest to the men who had earlier finished dismantling the remaining wagons at the time.

There were eight sidings within the area next to the filled-in West Pond site. These were originally used for the storage of coal wagons waiting to be unloaded at the various tipping lines located at the southern-most part of No. 1 Dock. Once the West Pond site itself was filled in to the north of these sidings, more

A grave time in the history of Barry scrapyard and the efforts to preserve all the engines. July 1980 saw the cutting up of two locomotives due to the lack of wagon contracts. Here, No. 92085, is almost unrecognisable after attention from the cutting torches. GWR large prairie No. 4156 was also dealt with that month bringing fears to the Barry Rescue project's ambitions to save all the locomotives. *Roger Hardingham*

lines were laid which eventually became the cutting up areas for both J O williams for a short period and then of course Woodham Brothers.

The numbers of locomotives reached their maximum around 1968 and occupied the old tips sidings closest to the old Barry Works and the eight sidings in the lower area by the old West Pond. Numbers in the top yards gradually reduced with engines moving out of Barry following purchase and as a result of this, by the late 1970s, the top yards were emptied and all the remaining engines were stored at the lower West Pond site.

Many of the first arrivals of locomotives, mostly from the Western Region, would actually steam into the yards and their fires left to go out. Others were towed in groups by one of the engines destined for scrap or by a diesel locomotive and observations are often recalled of these processions through Gloucester or Bath. Many of the Great Western types would still have their numberplates in situ on the smokebox door and on the cab sides. Southern types would also have their smokebox door numberplates still on and in most cases all the copper and brass fittings were in place just as they were when in service on BR. In the late 1960s these non ferrous parts were removed by Woodhams' men as they were beginning to disappear to 'collectors'. Fortunately, for preservationists, the tender axle-box brasses were kept by Woodhams in a shed near their offices in Thompson Street which were then offered back to the new owners of the tender as part of the purchase price.

A question of too many engines and not enough tenders

All the tender locomotives purchased by Woodhams from BR arrived with their tenders attached. As we know, Woodham Brothers were in the scrap business and when a new business opportunity arose, they were quick to capitalise on it. In the late 1960s there were many BR Standard and ex Southern Pacifics on the site at West Pond and these would produce a quick turnover in income for Woodham Metals Limited. The large tenders on these locomotives and on some GW 2-8-0 engines, proved ideal for re-use as carriers and many of them were sold to various steel producing works in the local area. Thus these tenders were stripped of their tanks and ended their days carrying ingots around these steel works, a far cry from their heyday's on the main lines of Britain.

As preservation attempts began to gather pace from the early 1970s onwards, the lack of tenders produced a stumbling block, but it did prove to everyone that Dai Woodham was in the business of scrapping and not retaining locomotives for preservation. If he was attempting the latter course, he would never have sold off large numbers of tenders.

Research shows that tenders started to either disappear or get separated from engines from 1969. By 1973 some 49 had left their mother locomotive and so as various locos were reserved or sold, they had to locate a tender from another engine. No. 71000 *Duke of Gloucester* was one famous example where it had lost its tender to a steel works and the new owners commandeered another from a 9F in the yard.

One locomotive which lost its tender to a steel works was No. 71000 *Duke of Gloucester.* This view in 1973 shows the unique locomotive shortly before removal to Loughborough which would be with a 9F tender from an engine elsewhere in the yard.

Roger Hardingham

Preservation mania

As soon as the last scheduled BR steam train ran in August 1968, Britain's huge enthusiast following had to contend themselves with a new-look railway. The hobby had changed dramatically over a number of years and the seeds were being sown in several parts of Britain to create preserved railways out of redundant routes following the Beeching axe of 1963. These railways needed motive power and although some steam locomotive stock was purchased in the closing years of steam directly from BR more would be required to sustain a timetable. The solution to that demand was at Barry. Woodham Brothers decided not cut up all their locomotives, unlike their business rivals around the UK who did cut up all of their engines. So the town of Barry in South Glamorgan provided the answer for the growing demand from preservation.

The fire in No. 70013 *Oliver Cromwell* was hardly cold after operating the final BR end of steam special on 11th August, when the first Barry engine was purchased (No. 31618) and No. 43924 became the first to move out, in September 1968. There followed 30 years of individuals, societies and groups reserving, buying and moving out locomotives to all parts of Britain.

The peak years for removals were between 1973 and 1975 when 51 locomotives left Barry and a new lease of life. This period in the 1970s was a very difficult one economically, but the number of new preserved railway lines springing up around the country continued nonetheless. The largest number of engines to leave Barry in a single year was in 1981 when 21 departed from the yard.

A locomotive not only devoid of its tender, but it smokebox door and centre driving wheels which had been cut through owing to a shunting accident. No. 45699 *Galatea* is seen in the yard in June 1976. It moved in April 1980 to Carnforth, then to the Severn Valley Railway before going back to Carnforth for full restoration. *David Olsen-Hopper*

Locomotives saved from Woodham Brothers yard at Barry, South Glamorgan

GREAT WESTERN RAILWAY

No.	Name	Date Built	Date Withdrawn	BARRY Arrived	BARRY Departed
Churchward 2800 Class 2-8-0					
2807		10/1905	3/1963	11/1963	6/198
2857		5/1918	4/1963	11/1963	8/197:
2859		5/1918	12/1964	3/1965	10/198'
2861		6/1918	3/1963	11/1963	2/198
2873		11/1918	12/1964	3/1965	3/198.
2874		11/1918	5/1963	11/1963	8/198
Collett 2884 Class 2-8-0					
2885		3/1938	1/1964	4/1964	3/198
Collett 5700 Class 0-6-0PT					
3612		3/1939	10/1964	3/1965	12/19'
3738		9/1937	8/1965	10/1965	4/197
Collett 2884 Class 2-8-0					
3802		12/1938	8/1965	10/1965	9/198
3803		1/1939	7/1963	11/1963	11/198
3814		3/1940	12/1964	3/1965	7/198
3822		4/1940	1/1964	4/1964	5/197
3845		4/1942	6/1964	10/1964	11/198

A line of Great Western types in the top yard which was used from 1965 to store engines awaiting scrapping. In the event most of these pictured in 1964 would survive.

No.	Name	Date Built	Date Withdrawn	BARRY Arrived	Departed
Collett 2884 Class 2-8-0					
3850		6/1942	8/1965	10/1965	4/1984
3855		10/1942	8/1965	10/1965	8/1987
3862		11/1942	2/1965	7/1965	4/1989
Collett 5101 Class 2-6-2T					
4110		10/1936	6/1965	8/1965	5/1979
4115		10/1936	6/1965	8/1965	3/1988
4121		12/1937	6/1965	8/1965	2/1981
4141		8/1946	3/1963	11/1963	1/1973
4144		9/1946	6/1965	8/1965	4/1974
4150		6/1947	6/1965	8/1965	5/1974
4160		9/1948	6/1965	8/1965	8/1974
Churchward 4200 Class 2-8-0T					
4247		3/1916	4/1964	11/1964	4/1985
4248		4/1916	5/1963	11/1963	5/1986
4253		3/1917	4/1963	7/1963	8/1987
4270		12/1919	9/1962	7/1963	7/1985
4277		4/1920	6/1964	9/1964	6/1986
Churchward 4500 Class 2-6-2T					
4561		10/1924	5/1962	9/1962	9/1975
4566		10/1924	4/1962	8/1962	7/1970
Churchward 4575 Class 2-6-2T					
4588		3/1927	7/1962	10/1962	10/1970
Collett 5700 Class 0-6-0PT					
4612		2/1942	8/1965	10/1965	1/1981
Collett 4900 Class 4-6-0					
4920	*Dumbleton Hall*	3/1929	12/1965	2/1966	6/1976
4930	*Hagley Hall*	5/1929	12/1963	6/1964	1/1973
4936	*Kinlet Hall*	6/1929	1/1964	4/1964	5/1981
4942	*Maindy Hall*	7/1929	12/1963	6/1964	4/1974
4953	*Pitchford Hall*	8/1929	5/1963	11/1963	2/1984
4979	*Wootton Hall*	2/1930	12/1963	6/1964	10/1986
4983	*Albert Hall*	1/1931	12/1963	6/1964	10/1970

No.	Name	Date Built	Date Withdrawn	BARRY Arrived	Departed
Collett 4073 Class 4-6-0					
5029	*Nunney Castle*	5/1934	12/1963	6/1964	5/1976
5043	*Earl of Mount Edgcumbe*	3/1936	12/1963	6/1964	9/1973
5051	*Earl Bathurst*	5/1936	5/1963	11/1963	2/1970
5080	*Defiant*	5/1939	4/1963	11/1963	8/1974
Churchward 5100 Class 2-6-2T					
5164		11/1930	4/1963	11/1963	1/1973
5193		10/1934	6/1962	10/1962	8/1979
5199		11/1934	3/1963	11/1963	7/1985
Collett 5205 Class 2-8-0T					
5224		5/1924	4/1963	11/1963	10/1978
5227		9/1924	2/1963	7/1963	2/1988
5239		8/1924	4/1963	11/1963	6/197?
Churchward 4300 Class 2-6-0					
5322		8/1917	4/1964	11/1964	3/196?
Churchward 4575 Class 2-6-2T					
5521		12/1927	4/1962	8/1962	9/1975
5526		5/1928	6/1962	10/1962	7/1985
5532		6/1928	7/1962	10/1962	4/1981
5538		7/1928	10/1961	3/1962	2/1987
5539		7/1928	4/1962	8/1962	3/1988
Churchward 4575 Class 2-6-2T					
5541		8/1928	7/1962	12/1962	10/197.
5542		7/1928	12/1961	3/1962	9/1975
5552		11/1928	10/1960	1/1961	6/198?
5553		11/1928	11/1961	3/1962	1/1990
5572		2/1929	4/1962	8/1962	8/197?
Collett 5600 Class 0-6-2T					
5619		3/1925	6/1964	9/1964	5/197?
5637		9/1925	6/1964	9/1964	8/1974
5643		10/1925	7/1963	11/1963	9/197?
5668		6/1926	9/1964	11/1964	8/198?

No.	Name	Date Built	Date Withdrawn	BARRY Arrived	Departed
Collett 4900 Class 4-6-0					
5900	*Hinderton Hall*	3/1931	12/1963	6/1964	6/1971
5952	*Cogan Hall*	12/1935	6/1964	11/1964	9/1981
5967	*Bickmarsh Hall*	3/1937	6/1964	8/1964	8/1987
5972	*Olton Hall*	4/1937	12/1963	6/1964	5/1981
Collett 6000 Class 4-6-0					
6023	*King Edward II*	6/1930	6/1962	12/1962	12/1984
6024	*King Edward I*	6/1930	6/1962	12/1962	3/1973
Collett 5600 Class 0-6-2T					
6619		1/1928	3/1963	11/1963	10/1974
6634		8/1928	4/1964	11/1964	6/1981
6686		10/1928	4/1964	11/1964	2/1988
6695		10/1928	7/1964	9/1964	5/1979
Hawksworth 6959 Class 4-6-0					
6960	*Raveningham Hall*	3/1944	6/1964	8/1964	10/1972
6984	*Owsden Hall*	2/1948	12/1965	2/1966	10/1986
6989	*Wightwick Hall*	3/1948	6/1964	8/1964	1/1978
6990	*Witherslack Hall*	4/1948	12/1965	2/1966	11/1975
Collett 4073 Class 4-6-0					
7027	*Thornbury Castle*	8/1949	12/1963	6/1964	8/1972
Collett 7200 Class 2-8-2T					
7200		8/1934	7/1963	11/1963	9/1981
7202		9/1934	6/1964	8/1964	4/1974
7229		8/1935	8/1964	11/1964	10/1984
Churchward 4300 Class 2-6-0					
7325		2/1932	4/1964	11/1964	8/1975
Collett 7800 Class 4-6-0					
7802	*Bradley Manor*	1/1938	11/1965	7/1966	1/1979
7812	*Erlestoke Manor*	1/1939	11/1965	5/1966	5/1974
7819	*Hinton Manor*	2/1939	11/1965	5/1966	1/1973
7820	*Dinmore Manor*	11/1950	11/1965	5/1966	9/1979
7821	*Ditcheat Manor*	11/1950	11/1965	5/1966	6/1981
7822	*Foxcote Manor*	12/1950	11/1965	5/1966	1/1975
7827	*Lydham Manor*	12/1950	10/1965	5/1966	6/1970
7828	*Odney Manor*	12/1950	10/1965	5/1966	6/1981

No.	Name	Date Built	Date Withdrawn	BARRY Arrived	Departed
Hawksworth 6959 Class 4-6-0					
7903	*Foremarke Hall*	4/1949	6/1964	1/1964	6/1981
7927	*Willington Hall*	10/1950	12/1965	2/1966	2/1988
Hawksworth 9400 Class 0-6-0PT					
9466		2/1952	7/1964	11/1964	9/1975
Collett 5700 Class 0-6-0PT					
9629		12/1945	10/1964	3/1965	5/1981
9681		5/1949	8/1965	10/1965	10/1975
9682		5/1949	8/1965	10/1965	11/1982

TOTAL LOCOMOTIVES = 98

SOUTHERN RAILWAY

No.	Name	Date Built	Date Withdrawn	BARRY Arrived	Departed
Urie S15 Class 4-6-0					
30499		5/1920	1/1964	6/1964	11/1983
30506		10/1920	1/1964	6/1964	4/1976
Maunsell Q Class 0-6-0					
30541		2/1939	11/1964	2/1965	5/1974
Maunsell S15 Class 4-6-0					
30825		4/1927	1/1964	6/1964	11/1986
30828		7/1927	1/1964	6/1964	3/1981
30830		8/1927	7/1964	12/1964	9/1987
30841		7/1936	1/1964	6/1964	9/1972
30847		12/1936	1/1964	6/1964	10/1978
Maunsell U Class 2-6-0					
31618		10/1928	1/1964	6/1964	1/1969
31625		3/1929	1/1964	6/1964	3/1980
31638		5/1931	1/1964	6/1964	7/1980
31806		6/1928	1/1964	6/1964	10/1976
Maunsell N Class 2-6-0					
31874		9/1925	3/1964	6/1964	3/1974
Bulleid West Country & Battle of Britain Class 4-6-2					
34007	*Wadebridge*	8/1945	10/1965	5/1966	5/1981
34010	*Sidmouth*	9/1945	3/1965	9/1965	1/1982
34016	*Bodmin*	11/1945	6/1964	11/1964	7/1972

Above: Bulleid Pacific No. 34072 *257 Squadron* in the lower yard soon after arrival in 1964. In total, 18 Bulleid light pacifics and 10 of the Merchant Navy class were to leave the yard at Barry for preservation. No. 34072 is now on the Swanage Railway.

Below: Urie S15 No. 30499 had to wait another seven years before being rescued. As with other classes sent to Barry such as the S&D 2-8-0s, the Q class, *Duke of Gloucester* and others, had it not been for Woodhams, these Urie engines would be extinct today.

No.	Name	Date Built	Date Withdrawn	BARRY Arrived	Departed
34027	*Taw Valley*	4/1946	8/1964	12/1964	4/1980
34028	*Eddystone*	5/1946	5/1964	11/1964	5/1986
34039	*Boscastle*	9/1946	5/1965	9/1965	1/1973
34046	*Braunton*	11/1946	10/1965	1/1966	7/1988
34053	*Sir Keith Park*	1/1947	10/1965	3/1966	6/1984
34058	*Sir Frederick Pile*	3/1947	10/1964	4/1965	7/1986
34059	*Sir Archibald Sinclair*	4/1947	5/1966	10/1966	10/1979
34067	*Tangmere*	9/1947	11/1963	4/1965	1/1981
34070	*Manston*	1/1947	8/1964	12/1964	6/1983
34072	*257 Squadron*	4/1948	10/1964	3/1965	11/1984
34073	*249 Squadron*	5/1948	6/1964	4/1965	2/1988
34081	*92 Squadron*	9/1948	8/1964	4/1965	11/1976
34092	*City of Wells*	9/1949	11/1964	3/1965	10/1971
34101	*Hartland*	2/1950	7/1966	10/1966	7/1978
34105	*Swanage*	3/1950	10/1964	2/1965	3/1978

Bulleid Merchant Navy Class 4-6-2

No.	Name	Date Built	Date Withdrawn	BARRY Arrived	Departed
35005	*Canadian Pacific*	12/1941	10/1965	1/1966	3/1973
35006	*P & O S.N.Co*	12/1941	8/1964	12/1964	3/1983
35009	*Shaw Savill*	6/1942	9/1964	12/1964	2/1989
35010	*Blue Star*	7/1942	9/1966	3/1967	1/1985
35011	*General Steam Navigation*	12/1944	2/1966	6/1966	3/1989
35018	*British India Line*	5/1945	8/1964	12/1964	3/1980
35022	*Holland-America Line*	10/1948	5/1966	10/1966	3/1986
35025	*Brocklebank Line*	11/1948	9/1964	12/1964	2/1986
35027	*Port Line*	12/1948	9/1966	3/1967	12/1982
35029	*Ellerman Lines*	2/1949	9/1966	3/1967	1/1974

TOTAL LOCOMOTIVES = 41

A chilling reminder that not all Bulleid Pacifics would escape the cutters torches. Here, the broken wheels of either No. 34045 or 34094 lay on the ground at Barry in the 1970s. They were both cut up in 1965.

LONDON MIDLAND & SCOTTISH RAILWAY

No.	Name	Date Built	Date Withdrawn	BARRY Arrived	BARRY Departed
Ivatt 2MT Class 2-6-2T					
41312		5/1952	7/1967	1/1968	8/1974
41313		5/1952	10/1965	2/1966	7/1975
Stanier 5FH Class 2-6-0					
42765		8/1927	12/1966	7/1967	5/1978
42859		3/1930	12/1966	6/1967	12/1986
Stanier 5FS Class 2-6-0					
42968		1/1934	12/1966	6/1967	12/1973
Fowler (Midland) 4F 0-6-0					
43924		10/1920	6/1965	9/1965	9/1968
44123		7/1925	6/1965	8/1965	12/1981
44422		10/1927	6/1965	8/1965	5/1977
Stanier 5P5F Class 4-6-0					
44901		10/1945	8/1965	1/1966	2/1988
45163		8/1935	5/1965	1/1966	1/1987
45293		12/1936	8/1965	1/1966	12/1986
45337		4/1937	2/1965	1/1966	5/1984
45379		7/1937	7/1965	10/1965	5/1974
45491		12/1943	7/1965	1/1966	7/1981
Stanier 5XP Class 4-6-0					
45690	*Leander*	3/1936	3/1964	6/1964	5/1972
45699	*Galatea*	4/1936	11/1964	5/1965	4/1980
Ivatt 2MT 2-6-0					
46428		12/1948	11/1966	9/1967	10/1979
46447		3/1950	12/1966	6/1967	6/1972
46512		12/1952	11/1966	6/1967	5/1973
46521		2/1953	10/1966	3/1967	3/1971
Fowler 3F 'Jinty' 0-6-0					
47279		4/1924	12/1966	6/1967	8/1979
47298		12/1924	12/1966	6/1967	7/1974
47324		6/1926	12/1966	6/1967	2/1978
47327		7/1926	12/1966	1/1968	7/1970

No.	Name	Date Built	Date Withdrawn	BARRY Arrived	Departed
47357		7/1926	12/1966	11/1967	7/1970
47406		11/1926	12/1966	6/1967	6/1983
47493		2/1928	12/1966	6/1967	12/1972
Stanier 8F Class 2-8-0					
48151		9/1942	1/1968	9/1968	11/1975
48173		7/1943	7/1965	10/1965	9/1988
48305		11/1943	1/1968	9/1968	11/1985
48431		3/1944	5/1964	8/1964	5/1972
48518		9/1944	7/1965	10/1965	2/1988
48624		12/1943	7/1965	10/1965	7/1981
Fowler 7F Class 2-8-0					
53808		7/1925	2/1964	6/1964	10/1970
53809		7/1925	6/1964	8/1964	12/1975

TOTAL LOCOMOTIVES = 35

LONDON & NORTH EASTERN RAILWAY

Thompson B1 Class 4-6-0

No.	Name	Date Built	Date Withdrawn	BARRY Arrived	Departed
61264		12/1947	11/1965	9/1968	7/1976

TOTAL LOCOMOTIVES = 1

BRITISH RAILWAYS STANDARD

8P Class 4-6-2

No.	Name	Date Built	Date Withdrawn	BARRY Arrived	Departed
71000	*Duke of Gloucester*	5/1954	11/1962	10/1967	4/1974

5MT Class 4-6-0

No.	Name	Date Built	Date Withdrawn	BARRY Arrived	Departed
73082	*Camelot*	7/1955	6/1966	10/1966	10/1979
73096		12/1966	11/1967	2/1968	7/1985
73129		8/1956	12/1967	2/1968	1/1973
73156		12/1956	11/1967	2/1968	10/1986

4MT Class 4-6-0

No.	Name	Date Built	Date Withdrawn	BARRY Arrived	Departed
75014		12/1951	12/1966	10/1967	2/1981
75069		9/1955	9/1966	6/1967	3/1973
75078		1/1956	7/1966	10/1966	6/1972
75079		1/1956	11/1966	4/1967	3/1982

Above: One of two S&D 2-8-0 locomotives to arrive at Barry. No. 53808 pictured on 14th September 1968. It would be preserved at the West Somerset Railway. *David Knapman* *Below:* Black Five No. 45293 in June 1976 before it left for the Colne Valley Railway in December 1986. *David Olsen-Hopper*

No.	Name	Date Built	Date Withdrawn	BARRY Arrived	Departed
4MT Class 2-6-0					
76017		6/1953	7/1965	1/1966	1/1975
76077		12/1956	12/1967	9/1968	5/1987
76079		2/1957	12/1967	9/1968	7/1974
76084		4/1957	12/1967	9/1968	3/1983
2MT Class 2-6-0					
78018		3/1954	11/1966	6/1967	11/1978
78019		3/1954	11/1966	6/1967	3/1973
78022		5/1954	9/1966	3/1967	6/1975
78059		9/1956	11/1966	6/1967	5/1983
4MT Class 2-6-4T					
80064		6/1953	8/1965	10/1965	2/1965
80072		11/1953	7/1965	1/1966	7/1988
80078		2/1954	7/1965	6/1966	9/1976
80079		3/1954	7/1965	1/1966	5/1971
80080		3/1954	7/1965	1/1966	11/1980
80097		12/1954	7/1965	1/1966	5/1985
80098		12/1954	7/1965	1/1966	11/1984
80100		1/1955	7/1965	1/1966	10/1978
80104		3/1955	7/1965	1/1966	9/1984
80105		4/1955	7/1965	1/1966	10/1973
80135		4/1956	7/1965	1/1966	4/1973
80136		5/1956	7/1965	6/1966	8/1979
80150		12/1956	10/1965	1/1966	2/1988
80151		1/1957	5/1967	9/1967	3/1975
9F Class 2-10-0					
92134		5/1957	12/1966	7/1967	12/1980
92207		6/1959	12/1964	3/1965	10/1986
92212		9/1959	1/1968	9/1968	9/1979
92214		10/1959	8/1965	10/1965	12/1980
92219		1/1960	8/1965	10/1965	5/1985
92240		10/1958	8/1965	11/1965	10/1978
92245		11/1958	12/1964	3/1965	2/1988

TOTAL LOCOMOTIVES = 38

TOTAL OF ALL GROUPS = 213

Locomotives which have departed for preservation

s = locomotive steamed. m = used on main line * = never to steam again

1   s   43924   Purchased by the Midland 4F Preservation Society and moved to the Keighley & Worth Valley Railway at Haworth. The locomotive has the distinction of being the very first to leave the yard in September 1968, just a few weeks after the final British Rail steam train ran. Originally restored to LMS livery as No. 3924, it was later given a BR livery as No. 43924. Currently undergoing a full overhaul at Haworth with a boiler overhaul at Crewe.

2   s   31618   Originally purchased by the Southern Mogul Preservation Society and transferred to New Hythe, Kent, by rail in January 1969. It was decided soon afterwards to move the locomotive to the Kent & East Sussex Railway where restoration was completed in SR olive green livery. In 1977 No. 1618 moved again to its current home at the Bluebell Railway where several overhauls took place to keep the locomotive in action. The Maunsell Locomotive Society is now the owner. Currently on static display awaiting overhaul.

3   s   5322   The first locomotive at Barry to be the subject of a preservation appeal. The national appeal for funds was not to succeed, resulting in a member of the Great Western Society purchasing No. 5322. It was restored at Caerphilly in South Wales and transferred to the GWS Didcot depot in 1973. After only a few years in steam it laid unused for many years until the engine was returned to its World War One appearance and finally ready to return to traffic in November 2008.

4   s m   5051   Firstly named *Drysllwyn Castle* but renamed *Earl Bathurst* in 1937, No. 5051 was shedded in South Wales for most of its career. In February 1970 it was moved to Didcot after purchase by a GWS member. The locomotive was returned to steam in January 1980 as *Drysllwyn Castle* and has been used on main line action since. Named as *Earl Bathurst* again, 5051 was in use on the main line until 2007 following an overhaul in early 2000. Out of traffic.

5   s   7827   *Lydham Manor*. Purchased originally for the Dart Valley Railway, No. 7827 was moved from Barry in June 1970 and, after restoration, entered service on the popular tourist Paignton - Kingswear line. The locomotive returned to service following a major overhaul in June 2005.

6   s   47327   First of the 'Jinty' locomotives to be retrieved from Barry, No. 47327 was purchased along with No. 47357 by Derby Corporation and moved in July 1970. Now a resident at the Midland Railway Centre, Butterley and under overhaul again following a long period in service. Now in Thomas livery.

7   s   47357   As with No. 47327, this locomotive was built at the North British Locomotive Company. After purchase by Derby Corporation it was restored and steamed at Butterley in 1973. Numbered 16440 and liveried in LMS crimson lake red, the locomotive has been a popular performer. Currently under overhaul.

8	s	4566	Purchased for the Severn Valley Railway and moved to Bewdley in 1970. Full restoration followed with No. 4566 proving a useful addition to the SVR fleet. Stored awaiting overhaul for many years, it was taken to Bridgnorth for overhaul in 2004, appearing in steam again in November 2006.
9	s	53808	First of the two Fowler 7F class 2-8-0s at Barry to depart. No. 53808 was bought by the Somerset & Dorset Circle and moved initially to Radstock in October 1970. A move to Washford on the West Somerset Railway followed to allow complete restoration, the locomotive steaming for the first time in 1987. This historic locomotive re-entered service for the 40th anniversary of the closure of the S&D in 2006 following a extensive overhaul.
10	s m	4983	*Albert Hall*. The first of sixteen 'Halls' at Barry to leave the yard for preservation. Purchased by the Birmingham Railway Museum and moved to Tyseley in October 1970. Further research in this locomotive's background revealed that No. 4983 was in fact No. 4965 *Rood Ashton Hall*. A return to steam was made in 2001 with the locomotive travelling far and wide over Network Rail. A fast-track overhaul took place in 2009 to re-new the locomotive's main line certificate.
11	s	4588	Purchased by the Dart Valley Railway and moved from Barry to Buckfastleigh in November 1970. The locomotive was speedily returned to steam for use on the Paignton - Kingswear Line and named *Trojan*. Now in store at Churston awaiting an overhaul.
12	s	46521	Purchased for the Severn Valley Railway, moving to the line in March 1971. Entry into service followed restoration to BR green livery. Now based at the Great Central Railway and under full overhaul.
13	s m	80079	Seen as being one of the most suitable locomotives to run on Britain's preserved lines, the Severn Valley Railway snapped up No. 80079 in May 1971. Following re-entry into service in 1977 the locomotive made its main line debut in April 1980 before its display at the Rainhill 150 celebrations. Currently awaiting an overhaul and on display at the National Railway Museum's Shildon exhibition.
14	s m	5900	*Hinderton Hall*. To expand the GWR collection at the GWS Didcot Railway Centre, No. 5900 was bought and moved in June 1971. Full restoration took place culminating in a main line tour in May 1976. On show at Didcot but out of service awaiting an overhaul.
15	s	5572	Synonymous with West Country branch lines, No. 5572 was an ideal choice for the GWS. Firstly moved in 1971 to a Taunton site, the locomotive was moved to Didcot for the completion of restoration. Currently a static exhibit.
16	s	5643	Originally purchased by the Eastern Valleys Railway Co. and moved to Cwmbran in September 1971. After the failure of this scheme, No. 5643 moved to far off Steamtown in Carnforth, Lancashire. Based at Haverthwaite, Cumbria from 1989 under the ownership of the Furness Railway Trust and restored, steaming in October 2005.

A GWR 'Hall' class and a SR 'U' class lined up against the wall of the old Barry Works.

17   s m   34092   *City of Wells*. Purchased by a group of members from the Keighley & Worth Valley Railway, No. 34092 made its way to Haworth in October 1971. After first steaming in 1977, its official re-entry into traffic came in April 1980. After ten years operation on the KWVR and many main line trips, the locomotive is now nearing the end of an extensive overhaul.

18   s m   45690   *Leander*. Having spent a greater part of its life at Bristol Barrow Road Depot, a short trip to Barry followed in 1964. A private purchaser arranged for its move in 1972 and full overhaul in British Rail's Derby Workshops. Its return to steam was in August 1973 after which many main line runs followed. *Leander* departed for the Severn Valley Railway in August 1980 for a full overhaul in the railway's own workshops at Bridgnorth. This Jubilee was purchased by Dr Peter Beet in the late 1990s and has just re-entered main line service, being based from Tyesley initially, then at Carnforth from 2008.

19   s   48431   Purchased for the Keighley & Worth Valley Railway and moved to Haworth in May 1972. Two major overhauls have been completed between 1972 and 1992, providing the railway with a solid addition to its motive power. Currently stored awaiting overhaul.

20   46447   Bought by the Ivatt Locomotive Trust and moved to the Buckinghamshire Railway Centre in June 1972. Now based at the Isle of Wight Steam Railway at Havenstreet and waiting full restoration.

21   s   75078   Purchased by the Standard 4 Preservation Society and moved to the Keighley & Worth Valley Railway at Haworth in June 1972. After full restoration No. 75078 entered service and was overhauled again in the mid 1990s. Currently undergoing a further overhaul.

22 s m 34016 *Bodmin.* Purchased by Mr. J. Bunch and Mr. R. Heather in 1972, the locomotive moved to the Quainton Road station site in July that year. Following the success of the Mid-Hants Railway scheme, No. 34016 moved to Alresford by road in November 1976. Entry into MHR service followed in September 1979 after a re-naming ceremony. In 1993 *Bodmin* was dismantled for a full general overhaul. Following major boiler repairs it returned to steam and occasional main line duties in 2000. Currently awaiting overhaul.

23 7027 *Thornbury Castle.* Purchased by the Birmingham Railway Museum and moved to Tyseley in August 1972. Sold to Pete Waterman and now stored at Crewe. One of the few early locomotives rescued from Barry in the early 1970s not to steam by the end of the 20th century.

24 s m 30841 Purchased by the Essex Locomotive Society and transported to the Stour Valley Railway at Chappel, Wakes Colne in September 1972. After an unsuccessful period of main line running, No. 841 (liveried in SR green and named *Greene King*) moved for a short period to the Nene Valley Railway, followed by a move to the North Yorkshire Moors Railway in 1978. Now of great use in Yorkshire, the locomotive was first painted in SR wartime black and in 1992 it was repainted in BR green and numbered 30841. A further overhaul has seen the locomotive transfer to number 30825 following the use of the spare frames from this canabalised locomotive from Barry.

25 s 5541 Purchased by the Prairie Fund, No. 5541 was moved to the Dean Forest Railway in October 1972. Steaming followed on 29th November 1975 and the locomotive entered service on the line. Returned to steam in August 1994 following another overhaul, 5541 has made a number of visits to other preserved railways including Bodmin & Wenford, Llangollen, and the Gwili. The boiler certificate expired early in 2004, and the loco is now under a major overhaul - its third on the Dean Forest Railway.

26 s m 6960 *Raveningham Hall.* Privately purchased and moved to Steamtown, Carnforth in October 1972. Following restoration No. 6960 made a main line trip and appeared at the Rail 150 event at Shildon. In 1977 the locomotive moved to the Severn Valley Railway after which a new owner, Mr Jeremy Hosking, took it to the Gloucester Warwickshire Railway. Currently away for overhaul at the West Somerset Railway at Minehead.

27 s 47493 After private purchase a move to Radstock followed in December 1972. In November 1973 No. 47493 was towed by rail to the East Somerset Railway at Cranmore where it was steamed in January 1976. This Jinty is now to be found at the Spa Valley Railway where it entered service in 2004.

28 s 4141 Purchased for the Severn Valley Railway and one of the few to be moved out of Barry by rail, on this occasion with Nos. 4930, 5164 and 7819 in January 1973. Based on the Llangollen Railway for several years, No. 4141 is currently at the Great Central Railway under the ownership of Dr John Kennedy and awaiting overhaul.

29 s m 4930 *Hagley Hall.* This locomotive was bought by a member of the Severn Valley Railway and moved to Bridgnorth in January 1973. Following overhaul, *Hagley Hall* was used extensively on the line and on main line tours. Once sited in a static condition at the shopping centre based at the old railway works at Swindon. Funds are being sought to return the loco to steam. It is now at the SVR awaiting an overhaul.

30 s 5164 Purchased by the 51XX Fund and moved to the Severn Valley Railway in 1973. Steamed in December 1979, No. 5164, along with ex-Barry SVR locomotives Nos. 2857, 4930 and 7812, it won the annual ARPS preservation award. Taken out of service for repair in 1984, No. 5164 is in service again.

31 s m 7819 *Hinton Manor.* One of three 'Manor' class locomotives at the Severn Valley Railway, *Hinton Manor* arrived on the line in January 1973. The locomotive returned to steam in 1977 and was associated with main line runs during the GWR 150 celebrations in 1985. Currently on display at the designer outlet at Swindon within the old GWR work's building.

32 s 73129 Because of the significance of being one of the steam locomotives built at Derby Works, Derby Corporation arranged the purchase and move from Barry to Derby by rail in January 1973. In 1975 No. 73129 was relocated to the Midland Railway Centre, Butterley. Steamed for the first time in May 2005, the first Caprotti valve geared Class 5 to operate since 1968.

33 s 34039 *Boscastle.* Privately purchased, *Boscastle* was moved by road to the Great Central Railway at Loughborough in January 1973. Since that date a lengthy restoration took place with the locomotive returning to steam in late 1992. Currently awaiting a full overhaul and stored at Loughborough.

34 s 80064 Purchased for use on the Dart Valley Railway, movement to the line followed in February 1973. Eight years of restoration resulted in a move from South Devon to the Bluebell Railway where it entered service. The Autumn of 1992 saw the return of the locomotive to Buckfastleigh following a ten year sojourn in Sussex. However, 80064 is now in store at the Bluebell awaiting overhaul.

35 s 78019 Purchased for the Severn Valley Railway and moved in March 1973. Moved for a complete overhaul to the Great Central Railway and steamed in 2004.

36 s m 6024 *King Edward I.* Sold by Woodham Bros. to the King Preservation Society and transported by road to Quainton Road in March 1973. This historic locomotive was given a major overhaul and a trial steaming and re-naming ceremony took place in 1989. No. 6024 was resident at the GWS Didcot Railway Centre from where it worked main line specials. Now based at Tyesley, *King Edward 1* is again regularly in use on the main line following an overhaul completed in 2004.

37 s m 75069 The ninth locomotive to leave for the Severn Valley Railway in March 1973. Full restoration to working order allowed the locomotive to run on BR main line specials as well as SVR metals. Currently under overhaul at Bridgnorth.

38   s m   35005   *Canadian Pacific*. Privately purchased for Steamtown, Carnforth, No. 35005 arrived in Lancashire in March 1973. Following many years stripped down for an overhaul, the locomotive moved to the Great Central Railway where it was subsequently steamed. Further work by owner Andrew Naish made this Bulleid available for main line use, but in 2002 was confined to branch line use by a new owner on the Mid-Hants Railway. Awaits an overhaul.

39   s m   80135   Purchased for use on the North Yorkshire Moors Railway and moved in April 1973 from Barry. During March 1980 No. 80135 was returned to steam but was dogged with firebox problems which necessitated the boiler going to the SVR for major repairs. The engine had the record for mileage in service on the railway.

40   s   5619   Purchased by Telford Development Corporation in May 1973. A seven year restoration followed resulting in a successful term of operation from 1981, and a period on hire to the Swanage Railway. Currently in use following a further overhaul at the Flour Mills site near Bream in the Dean Forest.

41   s   46512   Purchased for the Strathspey Railway and moved to the Severn Valley Railway for restoration in May 1973. Final restoration took place at Strathspey where it has been in operation. Currently waiting for overhaul.

42   s   5239   Now named *Goliath*. Sold to the Dart Valley Railway and moved to Devon in June 1973. No. 5239 entered service on the Paignton-Kingswear line in 1978. Currently in use.

43   s m   5043   *Earl of Mount Edgcumbe*. Originally named *Barbury Castle*, No. 5043 was purchased for the Birmingham Railway Museum, moving to Tyseley in September 1973. It was returned to steam in October 2008. No. 5043 is now restored to main line use.

44   s   80105   Purchased by the Scottish Railway Preservation Society, moving to Falkirk in October 1973. Overhauled and now in use at the Bo'ness Railway and on loan to the Strathspey Railway. The engine has also appeared at the Wensleydale Railway.

45   s m   42968   Following purchase by the Stanier Mogul Preservation Society, No. 42968 was moved to the Severn Valley Railway in December 1973. One of the most eagerly awaited locomotives for a return to steam, it was finally put into service in 1991. A further overhaul has seen the engine in use at the SVR.

46   s   76017   Purchased by the Standard 4 Preservation Group and originally moved to Quainton Road in January 1974. The locomotive subsequently moved to the Mid-Hants Railway in March 1978 and was returned to steam in 1984. Out of use by 1997, 76017 is undergoing a further overhaul at Ropley.

47   *   35029   *Ellerman Lines*. A locomotive definitely not capable of steaming in the future, it was purchased for the new National Railway Museum for exhibition as a cutaway exhibit. Restored in this condition at Market Overton from January 1974 and a popular attraction at York where visitors can see the inner workings of the engine.

A GW pannier tank looking a bit worse for wear is loaded up in the sidings close to the cutting line at the West Pond site. Most of the locomotives departed by road transport, although a few earlier departures did go out by rail, particularly those going to the Severn Valley and Didcot Railway Centre. This form of transport was stopped though as the engines started to deteriorate. One haulier, Mike Lawrence of Burnham, hauled out over 50 of the Barry engines.

48	s	31874	Named *Brian Fisk*, and for a while *Aznar Line*. Purchased by Mr J Bunch for use on the Mid-Hants Railway arriving there in March 1974. Restored in just two and a half years, No. 31874 hauled the re-opening train on the MHR on the 30th April 1977. The locomotive currently awaits an overhaul.
49	s	3738	Purchased for the GWS at Didcot and moved from Barry in April 1974. One of the quickest restorations followed, with No. 3738 steaming again just two years later. A further overhaul brought it into service in 1995 and another has seen No. 3738 in use from Easter 2007.
50	s	4144	Sold to the Great Western Society and moved to Didcot in April 1974. Overhauled at the GWS workshops and was in service at various times. Now awaiting a further overhaul.
51	*	4942	*Maindy Hall*. Bought by the Great Western Society and moved to Didcot by rail in April 1974. Early proposals to convert No. 4942 into a 'Saint' class locomotive (to be named *Lady of Legend*) have now, 35 years later, been realised, with the frames being prepared along with the boiler, at Riley Engineering at Bury. *Maindy Hall* itself will then be an extinct locomotive.

52		7202	Originally built as a 2-8-0T and numbered 5277, this locomotive was rebuilt as a 2-8-2T for use on coal traffic in South Wales. The GWS arranged purchase and removal in April 1974. Under long-term restoration at Didcot.
53	s m	71000	*Duke of Gloucester.* A unique locomotive when built in 1954, *Duke of Gloucester* hit the headlines again in 1974 when purchased by the Duke of Gloucester Trust. Deemed 'mission impossible' by many, the trust began one of the most difficult Barry restorations. Now a main line runner, No. 71000 has rightly joined the ranks of high performers, a fitting position for this truly unique locomotive. A second period of main line duties started in August 2004, followed by another term in 2010.
54	s	30541	The last of R E L Maunsell's designs to emerge from Eastleigh Works, the Q class numbered 20 in total. No. 30541 is the only survivor after being purchased by the Southern Q Fund and moved to Ashchurch, Gloucestershire, in April 1974. In 1978 it was moved again, this time to the Bluebell Railway for final restoration. Now owned by the Maunsell Locomotive Society, No. 30541 was a consistent runner on the line. Currently stored out of use.
55		45379	Purchased by a private group for the Bristol Suburban Railway Society and moved to Bitton in May 1974. Now owned by the Mid-Hants Railway and due to steam again in 2010.
56	s	7812	*Erlestoke Manor.* Purchased by the Erlestoke Manor Fund and moved out of Barry, firstly to Parkend and then to Ashchurch, Gloucestershire, in May 1974. A further move to the Severn Valley Railway was completed in April 1976 where a return to steam was effected in September 1979. Currently in operation following a return to steam in February 2008.
57		4150	Originally purchased and moved to the Dean Forest Railway in 1974 but despatched to the Severn Valley Railway in 1978. The last of the SVR Barry engines awaiting a return to steam.
58	s	47298	Purchased by the Liverpool Locomotive Preservation Group, moving to Southport in July 1974. After a return to steam in 1979, No. 47298 participated in the Rainhill 150 event in 1980. A move to the Llangollen Railway followed in 1983 where the tank has appeared in many liveries including much of its last years in blue for use as a 'Thomas' engine. Currently under overhaul.
59	s m	76079	Privately owned, No. 76079 moved to Steamport, at Southport in July 1974. Now on the East Lancashire Railway, the locomotive was purchased by Ian Riley and has seen extensive use on the main line. Bought in 2009 by the North Yorkshire Moors Railway.
60	s	4160	Initially moved to the Birmingham Railway Museum in August 1974, No. 4160 was sold and moved in May 1981 to the Plym Valley Railway. From there it was to move on to the West Somerset Railway, returning to steam. Overhauled again under contract at the South Devon Railway at Buckfastleigh, it is currently in use.

61	s	5637	In 1974 No. 5637 was purchased from Woodhams in Barry by the Birmingham Railway Museum and moved to Tyseley. From here, Thamesdown Borough Council purchased the locomotive, and it was moved to the Swindon & Cricklade Railway. Here, the 5637 Steam Locomotive Group purchased the locomotive and carried out complete restoration - a notable achievement, considering that there were no indoor facilities of any kind for this work. 5637 is at present on loan to the East Somerset Railway.
62	s m	5080	*Defiant.* Originally named *Ogmore Castle*, No. 5080 was moved to the Birmingham Railway Museum by rail with Nos. 5637 and 4160 in August 1974. Restored to main line condition, the locomotive was used on various special trains and resident at the GCR. Currently stored out of use.
63	s m	41312	Purchased for the Caerphilly Railway Society and moved to Caerphilly in August 1974. Privately purchased in the mid 1990s, 41312 is now based at the Mid-Hants Railway where it returned to steam in 2000 with some use on the main line. Currently awaiting another overhaul.
64	s	6619	Purchased privately for the North Yorkshire Moors Railway moving in October 1974. First steamed in 1984 and occasionally loaned out to other lines such as the Kent & East Sussex Railway in 1992. Overhauled again and in service.
65	s	7822	*Foxcote Manor.* Purchased by the Foxcote Manor Society and moved to Oswestry in January 1975. Restoration finally took place at the Llangollen Railway, where the locomotive now resides. A return to steam was made in September 1987 and a further overhaul in the late 1990s witnessed the locomotive in steam again from 1999. Currently awaiting another overhaul.
66	s	80151	Sold by Woodhams to the Stour Valley Railway, moving to Chappel & Wakes Colne in Essex in March 1975. Moved to the Bluebell Railway entering service in 2001. Boiler ticket expires in 2011.
67	s	78022	Purchased by the Standard Locomotive Preservation Society for use on the Keighley & Worth Valley Railway, arriving in June 1975. Fully restored to working order, entering service in 1992. Out of service awaiting overhaul.
68		41313	Purchased by the Ivatt Locomotive Trust, moving to Quainton Road Station in July 1975. During October 2006, the Ivatt Trust loaned the unrestored engine to the Isle of Wight Steam Railway where it will be restored in time.
69	s m	2857	Purchased by the 2857 Fund for the Severn Valley Railway and moved from Barry in August 1975 by rail with 7325. Restored in 1979 to working order and subsequently to main line condition, appearing at Newport hauling restored freight wagons during the GWR 150 event. No. 2857 has been loaned to various other railways including the Gloucestershire & Warwickshire Railway. Taken out of traffic in 1994, No. 2857 is currently due to steam again in 2010 following an extensive overhaul.

70 s m 7325 Purchased for the Severn Valley Railway, moving in August 1975. In 1992, when the engine was first returned to traffic, it assumed the identity of No. 9303, (the number first given to the locomotive when built), before reverting back to No. 7325 in 1993. As well as SVR services, this engine has also operated over main lines, working with LMS 2-6-0 No. 2968. These two engines, marked the return of steam to the Lickey Incline near Bromsgrove in 1997. Currently awaiting a full overhaul.

71 s 4561 Purchased by the West Somerset Railway Association and moved to the line in September 1975. Fully overhauled and steamed in 1989 on the WSR operating until 1998, after which it has been stored awaiting a further overhaul.

72 s 5521 Originally purchased for the West Somerset Railway but then moved to the Dean Forest Railway. Full restoration took place at Bill Parker's Flour Mill workshops for a steaming in 2006. The engine is unique in that it was fitted with an air pump and travelled to Poland. It steamed through Poland and Slovakia to Hungary in 2007, and back again in 2008 and in September 2007 piloted the Venice Simplon-Orient-Express on its way back from Istanbul to Venice! All quite a feat for an engine that languished in the sea air at Barry for 13 years.

73 s 5542 Bought for the West Somerset Railway and moved to Bishops Lydeard in September 1975. The locomotive entered service in 2002. Now in use at the Gloucester Warwickshire Railway.

The sole LNER-type locomotive to be despatched to Barry. No. 61264 latterly had the number 29 for use as a stationary boiler. It left Barry in 1976.   *Roger Hardingham*

74 s m   9466   Purchased for the Quainton Railway Society moving to Quainton in September 1975. Restored to main line condition and a regular performer at the now named Buckingham Railway Centre, No. 9466 ended its first period of use in 2001. However, a further overhaul was completed in 2004.

75 s   9681   Purchased by the Dean Forest Railway and moved to Norchard in October 1975. Restored to working order as the line's main locomotive in September 1984. In service again from March 2005 following a further boiler overhaul at the Flour Mills Works, Bream.

76 s   6990   *Witherslack Hall*. Purchased by the Witherslack Hall Locomotive Society and moved to the Great Central Railway in November 1975. Fully restored at Loughborough in 1986 but now awaiting a further overhaul.

77 s m   48151   Purchased privately and moved to the Yorkshire Dales Railway in November 1975. Restored to main line order at Wakefield making its debut in 1988. Operational from Carnforth for main line use.

78 s m   53809   Purchased privately and firstly moved to Kirk Smeaton for restoration. A move to Butterley followed for final assembly prior to an appearance at the Rainhill Celebrations in 1980. Various main line trips followed by this A further overhaul was completed by 2006. Now in service on the North Yorkshire Moors Railway.

79 s   30506   Bought by the Urie Locomotive Society in March 1973 just before VAT came into being. Moved to the Mid-Hants Railway in April 1976 after a ballot of its members. Following what was thought to be a serious fault in the boiler, 30506 received the one from No. 30825, still at Barry in 1981. Full restoration took place, the locomotive entering service in 1987 in SR green livery. A repaint into BR black followed in February 1993, followed by Southern 'sunshine' lettering in the late 1990s. Currently under overhaul again.

80 s   3822   After a stay of twelve years at Barry, the Great Western Society purchased and moved the locomotive in May 1976. Following an extensive overhaul, including the fabrication of a new front tubeplate, 3822 has been a popular attraction at Didcot and has been loaned to other railways. Available again following a further overhaul.

81 s m   5029   *Nunney Castle*. Purchased for the Great Western Society and moved to Didcot in May 1976. Restored to main line condition and a regular performer. Transfer of ownership took pace in 2004 to Jeremy Hoskings. Currently in use on the main line.

82 s   4920   *Dumbleton Hall*. Purchased by the Dumbleton Hall Preservation Society and moved to Buckfastleigh on the Dart Valley Railway in June 1976. It was fully restored and operated on the Paignton & Dartmouth Railway, 4920 is the oldest surviving 'Hall' class locomotive and is now based on the South Devon Railway. Currently stored at Buckfastleigh awaiting a further overhaul following withdrawal in 2000.

| 83 | s m | 61264 | Notable for being the only ex-LNER type to go to Barry and one of the last locomotives to arrive in the yard. 61264's survival is owed to its departmental use as a stationary boiler (No. 29). Purchased by the Thompson B1 Locomotive Society and moved to the Great Central Railway in July 1976. Major firebox and boiler repairs were carried out to enable the locomotive's steaming, repairs which it should be said are some of the most extensive ever carried out in preservation. Was in use on the main line but now based at Barrow Hill near Chesterfield. A major 10-year overhaul is underway with the boiler virtually completely dismantled at LNWR workshops at Crewe, where a new firebox has been constructed. |

| 84 | s | 80078 | Purchased by the Southern Steam Trust and moved to Swanage in September 1976. Following an amalgamation with Southern Locomotives Ltd in 1995 and the completion of sister loco 80104 in 1997, 80078's restoration progressed rapidly until completion in November 1999 when it became the 99th Barry engine to be returned to steam. Since then it has operated alongside 80104 on the Swanage Railway, as well as making occasional visits to other railways. |

| 85 | s | 31806 | Originally built as a 2-6-4T in 1926, 31806 was purchased for the Mid-Hants Railway, arriving at Alresford in October 1976. A remarkably fast eighteen-month restoration started in 1979 with the locomotive entering service on April 24th, 1981. About to enter traffic again in 2010 after overhaul to early BR livery at Ropley. |

| 86 | s | 34081 | *92 Squadron*. Purchased by the Battle of Britain Locomotive Preservation Society and moved to the Nene Valley Railway in November 1976. Restoration was completed and the locomotive has seen service at various sites including the North Norfolk Railway. Taken to the Nene Valley Railway in May 2010 for an overhaul. |

| 87 | s | 44422 | Purchased for the North Staffordshire Railway and moved to Cheddleton in April 1977. Steam tested in late 1989, No. 44422 (renumbered 4422 in LMS livery) was been loaned to the East Lancashire Railway, the North Yorkshire Moors Railway and the West Somerset Railway in recent years. Now back in steam following a further overhaul. |

| 88 | | 6989 | *Wightwick Hall*. Purchased for the Quainton Railway Society and moved to Quainton in January 1978. In an advanced state of restoration. |

| 89 | s | 47324 | Purchased by the Fowler 3F Society and firstly moved to the Mid-Hants Railway in February 1978. A further move took place to the Avon Valley Railway, and then was re-located to the East Lancashire Railway to finalise its overhaul. Entered service in January 2005. |

| 90 | s | 34105 | *Swanage*. Purchased by the 34105 Light Pacific Group for the Mid-Hants Railway, arriving at Alresford in March 1978. First steamed in July 1987, *Swanage* has been working regularly on the line and visited the Great Central Railway and Swanage Railway in 1993. Currently out of use and stored at Ropley. |

| 91 | s | 42765 | Purchased for the Keighley & Worth Valley Railway leaving Barry in April 1978. Restored on a private site and moved to the East Lancashire Railway for operation. Currently out of traffic awaiting overhaul. |

91 s 42765 Purchased for the Keighley & Worth Valley Railway leaving Barry in April 1978. Restored on a private site and moved to the East Lancashire Railway for operation. Currently out of traffic awaiting overhaul.

92 s 34101 *Hartland*. Purchased privately for the Peak Railway and originally moved to Shaws Metals Ltd. at Derby in July 1978. No. 34101 moved to the Great Central Railway where final restoration took place for steaming in 1993. A move to the North York Moors took place for an initial summer hire in 1995, but the locomotive has remained there. Now stored awaiting a further overhaul.

93 s 92240 Purchased by the BR Class 9 Preservation Group and moved to the Bluebell Railway in October 1978 - the first 9F class to depart Barry. Put back into working order in 1990, although making an appearance at the Railway's centenary cavalcade in 1982 (out of steam). No. 92240 is currently out of traffic awaiting overhaul.

94   80100 Purchased by the Brighton Standard 4 Tank Fund and moved to the Bluebell Railway in October 1978. Considered a long-term restoration project and still in Barry condition.

95 s 30847 The last 4-6-0 locomotive built by the Southern Railway, No. 30847 was purchased by the Maunsell Locomotive Society and moved to the Bluebell Railway in October 1978. Full restoration to SR green livery took place with the locomotive steaming in October 1992. Currently out of traffic undergoing an overhaul which is well advanced.

96 s 5224   Purchased for the Great Central Railway arriving at Loughborough in October 1978. Steamed in 1984 and extensively used on the line. Overhauled again and now to be seen in use at the Gloucester Warwickshire Railway and other railways, including the Mid-Hants Railway.

97   78018 Purchased for the Market Bosworth Light Railway scheme and moved to Shakerstone in November 1978. Resold to the Darlington Railway Preservation Society and under restoration at Darlington. In an advanced state of restoration.

98 * 3612   Purchased for the Severn Valley Railway and moved in December 1978. The Llangollen Railway purchased the cylinders and frames for use on their NCB-used Pannier No. 7754.

99 s 6695   Purchased by the Great Western Steam Preservation Group and moved to Swanage in May 1979. Now in service following the boiler being steam tested in April 2005.

100   4110   Purchased by the GWR Preservation Group arriving at Southall in May 1979. Awaiting final assembly at Tyesley.

101 s 47279 Purchased by the South Yorkshire 3F Trust and moved to the Keighley & Worth Valley Railway in August 1979. Last overhauled in 2001 and in service.

102 s 80136 Purchased by the North Staffordshire Railway moving to Cheddleton in August 1979. Restored for use and often operated at the West Somerset Railway.

103 s 5193 Purchased for Steamport Southport and moved to the depot in August 1979. This move was featured in a BBC Bristol production about Mike Lawrence Transport from Burnham in Somerset who moved many engines out of Barry. Re-sold to the West Somerset Railway for conversion to a 2-6-0 tender locomotive. Now numbered 9351. This new 'mogul' entered traffic in 2004.

104 s 7820 *Dinmore Manor.* Purchased for the Gwili Railway arriving in September 1979. Located at the Birmingham Railway Museum for a period then restored and steamed in 1995 for use on the West Somerset Railway. The locomotive was withdrawn in 2004 for a major overhaul.

105 s 92212 Purchased for the Great Central Railway by 92212 Holdings Ltd. arriving on the line in September 1979. Entered traffic in the mid 1990s but then sold to Jeremy Hosking and now based at the Mid-Hants Railway.

106 46428 Purchased by the Strathspey Railway arriving in Scotland in October 1979. Now located on the East Lancashire Railway after purchase in 1987. Awaiting restoration.

107 s 73082 *Camelot.* Purchased by the 73082 Camelot Locomotive Society and moved to the Bluebell Railway in October 1979. Full restoration to working order took place. After a 10-year period in service, the locomotive was withdrawn in June 2005 for a general overhaul.

108 s 34059 *Sir Archibald Sinclair.* Purchased by the Battle of Britain Locomotive Group and moved to the Bluebell Railway by road with No. 73082 in October 1979. Now in service following completion of its restoration in 2009.

109 s m 7802 *Bradley Manor.* A locomotive which spent some 20 years on the Cambrian Section until 1965. No. 7802 was purchased by the Erlestoke Manor Fund and moved in November 1979 with a view to a source of spares for No. 7812 at the Severn Valley Railway. In 1983 it was decided to restore the locomotive to full working order which was achieved in 1993. Coupled with a 4000-gallon Collet tender, it has seen extensive use on the SVR and the main line. A further overhaul brought the engine into use again in May 2002.

110 35018 *British India Line.* Privately purchased for the Mid-Hants Railway and moved to Alresford in March 1980. Some restoration has taken place, but the locomotive was moved in 2003 to Portland in Dorset for storage.

111 s m 31625 Purchased privately for the Mid-Hants Railway arriving in March 1980. Restored for use on the MHR. Stored for overhaul, its boiler is currently fitted to 'N' Class No. 31874 which is also out of traffic.

112 s m 34027 *Taw Valley*. Privately purchased initially for the North Yorkshire Moors Railway but then moved to Hull for restoration to working order. A further move to the Severn Valley Railway was made to finish off the work to main line standard. Since steaming in 1989, *Taw Valley* has experienced considerable main line use including in 1992 on the Bournemouth main line - the first steam to do so since 1967. Currently out of traffic, under overhaul at Bridgnorth.

113 45699 *Galatea*. Purchased by the owner of No. 45690 *Leander* and moved to Carnforth in April 1980. In store for spare parts at the Severn Valley Railway. Re-purchased in the late 1990s by the owner of West Coast Railway Co. at Carnforth, Currently well advanced in its restoration.

114 s 31638 Purchased for the Bluebell Railway and moved in 1980. Now in the care of the Maunsell Locomotive Society and in use after an extensive restoration which has included an ex-Schools Class tender being refitted for use with this mogul.

115 s m 80080 Privately purchased for the Peak Railway initially and moved to the line in November 1980. A move to the Midland Railway Centre followed with No. 80080 becoming a main line runner, travelling to all parts of the BR system, including Barry in 1991 and the Settle-Carlisle Railway in 1993. Currently under overhaul with the boiler outshopped from the Severn Valley Railway in June 2010.

116 92134 Purchased for the North Yorkshire Moors Railway and moved from Barry in December 1980. Removed to a site in Brightlingsea in Essex for restoration. Currently based at the Railway Age, Crewe for restoration on behalf of the Churnet Valley Railway. The only surviving single-chimneyed 9F in preservation.

117 s 92214 Purchased for the Peak Railway moving to Buxton in December 1980. Put into use following full overhaul at the Midland Railway Centre at Swanwick in 2004. Based at the North York Moors Railway from late spring 2010.

118 s m 34067 *Tangmere*. Privately purchased by Brian Pickett for the Mid-Hants Railway moving in January 1981 to Alresford. With a full overhaul at Swindon and then finally at Bury, and one of the most expensive in railway preservation, *Tangmere* is used mostly in the South of England on the main line, being based at Southall. Ownership has changed twice since the death of Brian Pickett in 2004.

119 s 4612 Purchased for the Keighley & Worth Valley Railway and moved in January 1981 and used as a source of spares only. Ownership changed to Ray and Elaine Treadwell in 1987 after which restoration took place at the Swindon Works site and Flour Mills in the Forest of Dean. This remarkable restoration allowed 4612 to enter service at the Bodmin & Wenford Railway, Cornwall.

120 4121 Purchased for the Dean Forest Railway moving to Norchard in February 1981. Moved to the Crewe Heritage Centre and then to Tyesley for restoration.

One of 17 'Hall' class engines to survive from Barry. No. 6990 *Witherslack Hall* at Barry before departure for Loughborough in November 1975.   *Roger Hardingham*

121 s m   75014   Purchased for the North Yorkshire Moors Railway moving in February 1981. Returned to steam in the mid 1990s, 75014 saw main line service including use on The Jacobite trains from Fort William to Mallaig. Now owned by the Paignton & Dartmouth Railway, and under full overhaul.

122 s m   30828   Purchased by the Eastleigh Railway Preservation Society and moved from Barry in March 1981. Eleven years of careful restoration followed with No. 828 appearing in steam at the BRML Eastleigh Works Open Day in September 1992. A main line steam test followed in February 1993 to enable turns later in the year. In use at Cranmore for a period and then Swanage, 30828 is currently at the Mid-Hants under overhaul.

123   2885   Purchased by the GWR Preservation Group and moved to Southall in March 1981. Long-term restoration project.

124   5532   Purchased for the Dean Forest Railway and moved to the line in April 1981, mainly for use as spares for its two other prairie tanks. The story of this engine is very much connected to No. 5538, also at Barry. The Llangollen Railway Great Western Locomotive Group wanted to buy a Small Prairie tank from Barry, and from those that remained chose 5538. However, as this had a cracked cylinder, the group exchanged the frames and some other parts with 5532 at the Dean Forest in 1989, as this was felt to be the most economic option. The numbers of engines are decided by their frames and therefore the Llangollen group became owners of 5532 when the exchange was made. Now under restoration at Llangollen.

125 s m   5972   *Olton Hall*. Purchased privately and moved to the Wakefield area in May 1981. A move to Carnforth was made for final assembly. Now famous for its role hauling the Hogwarts Express in the Harry Potter films.

126 s m   4936   *Kinlet Hall*. Purchased for the Peak Railway and moved in May 1981. Removed to Toddington for a while and then to the Llangollen Railway, final restoration took place at Tyesley with a return to steam in 2000.

127 s   34007   *Wadebridge*. Purchased for use on the scheme at the Plym Valley Railway moving from Barry in May 1981 to a private siding before movement to the PVR in March 1982. Restored at the Bodmin and Wenford Railway in Cornwall, a return to steam was accomplished in 2005. Now partly owned and run by the Mid-Hants Railway.

128   9629   Purchased for static display outside the Holiday Inn Hotel in Cardiff. Cosmetically restored at Carnforth after a move from Barry in May 1981, the engine arrived on its plinth in Cardiff in 1986. Donated to the Pontypool & Blaenavon Railway in 1995 where the chassis is being restored and missing parts being assembled for restoration, including a boiler (its display at the Holiday Inn was without this vital item). The aim is to use the boiler acquired from the Keighley and Worth Valley Railway which was historically off a Deans Goods engine but will be adapted to fit No. 9629.

129 s   7903   *Foremarke Hall*. Purchased for the Swindon & Cricklade Railway and moved to Blunsden in June 1981. Returned to steam in 2004 and in use currently at the Gloucester & Warwickshire Railway.

130 s   2807   The oldest locomotive out of 213 to survive at Barry. Purchased for the Gloucestershire & Warwickshire Railway leaving Barry in June 1981 for Toddington. The 1905-built engine was sent to the Birmingham Railway Museum for long-term restoration, No. 2807 then transferred to the Llangollen Railway for completion. Its operation at the Gloucester & Warwickshire line began on 16th July following its first steaming and testing on 18th May 2010 at Llangollen.

131   6634   Purchased for use at the Cranmore Railway in Somerset moving in June 1981. Under restoration at the Severn Valley Railway for Pete Waterman.

132 s   7821   *Ditcheat Manor*. Bought for the Gloucestershire & Warwickshire Railway leaving Barry for Toddington in June 1981. Restored at the Llangollen Railway, No. 7821 went on hire to the Great Central Railway. Now resident at the West Somerset Railway.

133 s   7828   *Odney Manor*. Purchased with No. 7821 for the G & WR moving in June 1981. Seen at work on the East Lancashire Railway for several years, *Odney Manor* moved to the West Somerset Railway. Undergoing a major overhaul.

134   45491   Purchased privately and moved to a site at Blackpool in July 1981. Now at the Midland Railway Centre and in an advanced state of restoration.

135 s 48624 Purchased for the Peak Railway and moved from Barry in July 1981 to Buxton for long-term restoration. The only Southern-built 8F in preservation, the loco was completed at the Rowsley depot on Peak Rail and moved under its own power for the first time on 25th April 2009. To be based at the Churnet Valley Railway, painted in LMS crimson livery.

136 5952 *Cogan Hall.* Purchased for the G & WR moving to Toddington in September 1981. Now awaiting restoration at the Llangollen Railway after purchased by the 6880 *Betton Grange* Society.

137 7200 Purchased for the Quainton Railway Society and moved to Quainton Road Station in September 1981. Still in ex-Barry condition.

138 44123 Purchased originally for the Mid-Hants Railway moving to Alresford in December 1981. Transfer from Barry necessitated a manual sideways move to a siding for loading onto a trailer. At the Avon Valley Railway at Bitton from May 1986, the locomotive awaits restoration.

139 75079 Purchased for the Plym Valley Railway and moved to Plymouth in March 1982. A package was presented to the Plymouth Lottery Sub-Committee, whereby funds could be used to purchase 75079 from Barry scrapyard and transport it to Plymouth. In return, on restoration of the locomotive, 75079 would be named *City of Plymouth.* On 12th March 1982 the locomotive left the yard. When 75079 was rescued no B.R. Standard tender was available, so an LMS 8F tender was rescued with the intention of re-building it to enable it to work with 75079. Now owned by the Mid-Hants Railway and in store at Ropley awaiting restoration.

140 34010 *Sidmouth.* Privately purchased for the North Yorkshire Railway and moved in November 1982. Moved to a private site in Middlesbrough for initial restoration, then purchased by Southern Locomotives Ltd., and stored at Sellindge, Kent. Now based at the Swanage Railway awaiting restoration.

141 s 9682 Purchased for the GWR Preservation Group at Southall, moving in November 1982. Restored from Barry condition to become the 100th locomotive to be fully restored from scrapyard condition. Its first run was in 2000 at the Swindon & Cricklade Railway. Now based at the Chinnor & Princes Risborough Railway. No. 9682's boiler certificate expired in Dec. 2009.

142 s 35027 *Port Line.* Privately bought and moved to the Swindon Works complex in December 1982. Full restoration took place to enable the locomotive to appear at the Woking 150 Celebrations in 1988. Following this event it was used at the Bluebell Railway until 2000, when a transfer to the Swanage Railway saw it in further use. Sold in 2005 to Jeremy Hosking with No. 35022 and taken to Southall for a full overhaul.

143 35006 *P & O SN Co.* Purchased by the 35006 P & O Locomotive Society for the Gloucestershire & Warwickshire Railway. No. 35006 left Barry for Toddington in March 1983. Restoration is at an advanced state.

| 144 | | 76084 | Purchased privately and moved to a private location at North Leverton in April 1983. Now owned by the 76084 Society and housed in Darlington for overhaul and eventual use on the North Yorks Moors Railway. |

144   76084   Purchased privately and moved to a private location at North Leverton in April 1983. Now owned by the 76084 Society and housed in Darlington for overhaul and eventual use on the North Yorks Moors Railway.

145   78059   Purchased for the Bluebell Railway and moved to Sheffield Park in May 1983. As no tender is available for No. 78059, a group at the Bluebell Railway is rebuilding it into a 2-6-2-T (as No. 82030).

146 s   34070   *Manston*. Purchased by the Manston Preservation Group and moved to the Richborough Power Station site in Kent in June 1983. Now owned by Southern Locomotives Ltd., and restored in the Works at Herston on the Swanage Railway. Brought into service in 2008.

147 s   47406   Purchased for the Peak Railway and moved to Buxton in June 1983. Since moved to the Great Central Railway where restoration was completed in 2009.

148   30499   The second of the two Urie S15s still in existence to be bought by the Urie Locomotive Society. No. 30499 was moved to Alresford on the Mid-Hants Railway in November 1983. At Bury for 13 years to allow a boiler swop with sister engine 30506 and now at the Mid-Hants Railway with work gradually progressing on the chassis.

149 s   3803   Purchased for the Dart Valley Railway and moved in November 1983. It was moved to the Birmingham Railway Museum, Tyseley, for restoration but was completed in the Works at Buckfastleigh on the South Devon Railway. Steamed in September 2006.

150 s   4953   *Pitchford Hall*. Purchased for the Dean Forest Railway and taken from Barry in February 1984. Moved to the Crewe Heritage Centre and then to Tyesley for full restoration. Returned to steam in January 2004 after a £1m restoration. Now owned by Dr John Kennedy.

151 s   3850   Bought for use on the West Somerset Railway and moved in April 1984 from Barry. Owned by the Dinmore Manor Locomotive Ltd., No. 3850 moved to Tyesley in 2003 for final restoration and was steam tested ready for entry into traffic in late summer 2005.

152 s   45337   Purchased for the East Lancashire Railway and transported to Bury in May 1984. Restoration took place at Bury and 45337 has seen many miles on preserved lines in recent years. Boiler ticket expired in August 2005. Expected to steam again in late 2010.

153   34053   *Sir Keith Park*. Purchased privately and moved to Hull in June 1984. Now owned by Southern Locomotives Ltd and under restoration at Swanage following many years stored at Sellindge. Expected to steam again in early 2011.

154 s   3802   Purchased privately and moved out of Barry in September 1984. First home was at Bodmin General Station in Cornwall but a move to the Llangollen Railway followed where restoration was completed. A steam test on the boiler out of the frames was made on 13th July 2005.

155 s   80104   Initially bought for use on the Swanage Railway, No. 80104 was moved in September 1984. Located at the Avon Valley Railway at Bitton for several years before overhaul by Southern Locomotives Ltd. and now to be seen working at Swanage.

156   7229   Purchased for the Plym Valley Railway and moved in October 1984. Now at the East Lancashire Railway and dismantled for restoration.

157 s   80098   Purchased for the Midland Railway Centre and moved in November 1984. Currently in use on long-term loan to the Churnet Valley Railway.

158 s   34072   *257 Squadron*. Purchased for use at the Swanage Railway and moved to Swindon Works in November 1984. Fully restored and was seen working not only on the Swanage line but on other sites around Britain. Now out of service and waiting for another overhaul.

159   6023   *King Edward II*. Initially moved to an area close to Temple Meads station at Bristol after sponsorship from Harvey's Bristol Cream and moved in December 1984. Then purchased by the Great Western Society for long-term restoration. New driving wheels have been cast to replace those cut away whilst at Barry in a shunting accident. Now nearing the end of its restoration which will see this second 'King' Class from Barry in BR blue livery.

A well-known example of the many inscriptions put on locomotives at Barry over the years. In the event No. 48305 didn't die and went to the GCR.

| 160 | | 35010 | *Blue Star.* Privately purchased by the British Enginemen's Steam Preservation Society and moved to North Woolwich in January 1985. Now resident at the Colne Valley Railway, Essex for restoration. |

160   35010   *Blue Star.* Privately purchased by the British Enginemen's Steam Preservation Society and moved to North Woolwich in January 1985. Now resident at the Colne Valley Railway, Essex for restoration.

161 s   4247   Purchased for use on the Cholsey & Wallingford Railway and moved from Barry in April 1985. Restored at the Gloucester Warwickshire Railway and at the Flour Mill workshops in the Dean Forest, No. 4247 was run in on the Avon Valley Railway before transfer to the Bodmin & Wenford Railway.

162   80097   Bought for use on the East Lancashire Railway by the Standard 4 Group, departing from Barry in May 1985. Restoration is proceeding within the group's own shed at Bury.

163   92219   Purchased originally for the Peak Railway but moved to the Midland Railway Centre in May 1985 where it is stored awaiting restoration.

164 s m   73096   Privately purchased for the Mid-Hants Railway and moved to Alresford in July 1985. Restoration proceeded to steaming in July 1993. Now in steam following a further overhaul, which saw the locomotive used on the main line. Currently in use at the MHR.

165 s   5199   After spending 22 years in Woodham's scrapyard, 5199 was purchased by the Great Western Steam Locomotive Group and moved to the Gloucestershire and Warwickshire Railway at Toddington in 1985 for restoration. In 1988 the owners moved the locomotive to Llangollen where work continued for a while. A further move in 1990 came when the frames moved to MOD Long Marston. Work progressed slowly, with re-wheeling taking place on 18th June 1995, the first major milestone in the restoration. 5199's first move under its own steam was in February 2003.

166 s   5526   Privately purchased and moved to the Gloucestershire & Warwickshire Railway in July 1985. Transferred to the Swindon Works complex for stripping down after a change of ownership. Eventually moved to the South Devon Railway for completion of its overhaul. In traffic at the SDR.

167   4270   Purchased for the Swansea Vale Railway and moved to Llansamlet, Swansea, in July 1985. Now to be located at the Gloucester Warwickshire Railway once restoration is completed at an off-site location.

168 s   48305   Purchased for the Great Central Railway and moved to their works at Loughborough in November 1985. Restoration was finished in time for a steaming in 1993. Famous in the yard at Barry for its smokebox door inscription, "Please Don't Let Me Die".

169   35025   *Brocklebank Line.* Purchased for use on the Great Central Railway and transferred to the line in February 1986. No. 35025 was destined to be the next in line for the cutter's torch in 1980 after the demise of 9F class No. 92085. After nearly 20 years at the GCR, the locomotive is now in store at Sellindge pending final restoration.

170   35022 *Holland America Line.* Privately purchased for eventual use on the
              Swanage Railway. Moved to Swanage in March 1986. Resited to Sellindge
              in Kent to join other Bulleid Pacifics there. Now owned by Jeremy Hosking
              and stored at Southall.

171 s 34028 *Eddystone.* Purchased by the 34028 Eddystone Locomotive Group and
              moved to Sellindge, Kent, in May 1986. Restoration was fully completed
              at the Swanage Railway where the locomotive entered service in 2004.

172   4248   Privately purchased and moved to a site at Brightlingsea, Essex for restoration
              in May 1986. Moved to the Swindon Works complex for display in 'Steam the
              Museum of the Great Western Railway'.

173 s 4277   Purchased privately by Pete Best for the Gloucestershire & Warwickshire
              Railway and removed from Barry to Toddington in June 1986. A move
              then took place to a private site to speed up restoration which was
              accomplished in 1996. Its inaugural working was on the Severn Valley
              Railway. Bought by the Paignton & Dartmouth Steam Railway in 2008.

174 s 5552   Purchased for the Bodmin & Wenford Railway and moved to Cornwall in
              June 1986. The boiler restoration took place at Roger Pridham's engineering
              near Tavistock. Now in service at the Bodmin & Wenford Railway, Cornwall.
              No. 5552 survived in the yard the longest having arrived in October 1960.

175   34058 *Sir Frederick Pile.* Purchased privately for the Avon Valley Railway,
              moving to Bitton in July 1986. A completely new tender is being built, including
              the casting of the correct pattern B.F.B. wheels. Once restored, only the
              wheels, frame and boiler will remain of the original locomotive

176   3814   Bought for use on the North Yorkshire Moors Railway by Peter Robinson,
              arriving in July 1986. Currently being restored in the deviation shed at
              Grosmont.

177   73156 Purchased for the East Lancashire Railway and moved in October 1986.
              Under restoration now at the Great Central Railway at Loughborough.

178   6984   *Owesden Hall.* Purchased privately and moved to a site at Bicester, Oxon,
              for restoration in October 1986. Now at Toddington, some restoration to
              the chassis has taken place and inspections made to the boiler and other parts.

179   4979   *Wootton Hall.* Purchased privately and moved to Fleetwood, Lancashire,
              in October 1986. Now under the ownership of the Furness Locomotive
              Group, No. 4979 went to at a site in Lytham before moving on to the Appleby
              Heritage Centre right next to the Settle-Carlisle line. No start has been made
              to restoration.

180   92207 Purchased for the East Lancashire Railway and moved in December
              1986. On 21st December 2005 the engine was re-located to Dorset at the
              Shillingstone Station Project. In the early stages of restoration.

181 s   30825   Remains moved from Barry to the North Yorkshire Moors Railway following the retrieval of the boiler for Urie S15 No. 30506 in 1981. The frames of 30825 have been used to re-frame No. 30841 on the North York Moors Railway, where the number of the 'S15' 30825 is now used and No. 30841 is rendered out of service.

182   45293   Purchased by the BR Enginemen's Steam Preservation Society for the Colne Valley Railway moving in December 1986. Under restoration.

183   42859   Privately purchased and moved to Hull in December 1986. Now at a site at RAF Binbrook, Lincolnshire.

184   45163   Privately purchased and moved to a site at North Woolwich in January 1987. Now at the Colne Valley Railway, Essex. Under restoration.

185   5538   Donated to the town of Barry by Dai Woodham for display on the seafront at Barry Island. After a few years it was then re-located to the Vale of Glamorgan Railway in 1997 and then later acquired by the Llangollen Railway Great Western Locomotive Group. The frames were swopped with those on No. 5532 at the Dean Forest line due to a cracked cylinder and other problems. The remains of this swop were considered a possibility for restoration and are now under re-building at the Dean Forest Railway with the boiler at the nearby Flour Mills.

186   76077   Purchased for the Gloucestershire & Warwickshire Railway moving to Toddington in May 1987. Awaiting restoration.

187   5967   *Bickmarsh Hall*. Purchased initially for use on the Pontypool & Blaenavon Railway moving in August 1987 with Nos. 3855, 5668, 4253 and 2874. Now at the Northampton & Lamport Railway, awaiting restoration

188   3855   Purchased for Pontypool & Blaenavon Railway leaving Barry in August 1987. Departed Blaenavon on 17th April 2008 for East Lancs Railway.

189   5668   Purchased for Pontypool & Blaenavon Railway. Left Barry in August 1987. This locomotive is currently being restored.

190   4253   Purchased for Pontypool & Blaenavon Railway. Left Barry in August 1987. Its whole operational life for the GWR and BR was from Newport shed.

191   2874   Purchased for Pontypool & Blaenavon Railway. Left Barry in August 1987. Sold to the West Somerset Railway and awaits restoration.

192   30830   Bought for eventual use on the Bluebell Railway. No. 30830 left Barry for Sussex in September 1987. Subsequently purchased for restoration at the North Yorkshire Moors Railway alongside S15s 30825 and 30841.

193   2859   Purchased for the Llangollen Railway by the The Llangollen Railway GWR Loco Group along with No. 5532 and moved from Barry in October 1987. Currently stored whilst restoration takes place on the small Prairie.

194   5227   Purchased for the Wales Railway Centre at Bute Road Station, Cardiff. No. 5227 was the first of ten locomotives to leave Barry in February and March 1988 for this site. On the failure of this scheme, the 'Barry 10' as they became known, moved to the Vale of Glamorgan Railway at Barry in 1996 for storage, initially to the old bus garage in Broad Street, then to the ex EWS wagon repair depot.

195   92245   Purchased for the Wales Railway Centre, Cardiff, moving in February 1988. Moved back to Barry for storage as one of the 'Barry 10'.

196   80150   Purchased for the Wales Railway Centre, Cardiff, moving in February 1988. Moved back to Barry for storage as one of the 'Barry 10'.

197   6686   Purchased for the Wales Railway Centre, Cardiff, moving in February 1988. Moved back to Barry for storage as one of the 'Barry 10'.

198 * 48518   Purchased for the Wales Railway Centre, Cardiff, moving to Bute Road in February 1988. Moved back to Barry for storage as one of the 'Barry 10'. 48518 was taken to the Llangollen Railway to be stripped down to allow the boiler to be used on the GWS project to build a County class locomotive at Didcot. The frames have gone in store to Doncaster and other parts to be used in the Patriot new-build project.

199   34073   *249 Squadron*. Purchased for the Brighton Works Project and moved to the Brighton site in February 1988. Purchased privately following this and moved to the Mid-Hants Railway. Currently stored at the East Lancs Railway after retrieval of some parts for 34067.

200   2861   Purchased for the Wales Railway Centre, Cardiff, moving in February 1988. Moved back to Barry for storage as one of the 'Barry 10'.

201 * 7927   *Willington Hall*. Purchased for the Wales Railway Centre, Cardiff, moving in February 1988. Moved back to Barry for storage as one of the 'Barry 10'. Now the subject of a deal for use in the building of a 'Grange' Class and 'County' class locomotive. A move for stripping down at the Llangollen Railway occurred in August 2005.

202   44901   Purchased for the Wales Railway Centre, Cardiff, moving in February 1988. Moved back to Barry for storage as one of the 'Barry 10' in 1996.

203   4115   Purchased for the Wales Railway Centre, Cardiff, moving in March 1988. Moved back to Barry for storage as one of the 'Barry 10'.

204   5539   Purchased for the Wales Railway Centre, Cardiff, moving in March 1988. Moved back to Barry for storage as one of the 'Barry 10'.

205   2873   Purchased for the Birmingham Railway Museum, Tyseley, for spares for similar locomotives. Left Barry in March 1988. However, a move to the South Devon Railway was subsequently made.

206 s 80072 Bought by the Llangollen Standard Four Project and moved from Barry in July 1988 to Swindon. A group of members purchased the locomotive in 1991, and restoration continued at both Swindon and Llangollen. Amongst items requiring renewal was a wheelset as one of the original wheels had been cut through after a derailment at Barry. In 1995 the engine moved to Llangollen for the later phases of restoration which was completed in 2009.

207 s 34046 *Braunton.* Purchased for the Brighton Works Project and moved to Brighton in July 1988. Following the collapse of the project in Brighton, *Braunton* was bought by Jeremy Hosking and moved to Williton on the West Somerset Railway for an extensive overhaul. Returned to steam in 2008.

208 48173 Purchased for the Avon Valley Railway at Bitton and moved from Barry in September 1988. Now sited at the Churnet Valley Railway awaiting restoration.

209 35009 *Shaw Savill.* Purchased for the Brighton Works Project and moved to Brighton in February 1989. This scheme failed and the engine changed ownership. Stored outside the new Swindon Works shopping complex until 2003 when it was sold again to Ian Riley and moved to Bury. Stored awaiting restoration.

210 35011 *General Steam Navigation.* Purchased for the Brighton Works Project and moved to Brighton in March 1989. It was then at a site in RAF Binbrook, Lincolnshire before moving again to Sellindge in Kent under the owners name of 'ACE Locomotives'. No. 35011 was moved temporarily to Williton on the West Somerset Railway to give up a set of wheels to help in the restoration of Bulleid No. 34046 *Braunton.*

211 3862 Bought for the Northampton & Lamport Railway at Chapel Brampton by the LNWR Preservation Society in 1987, departed from Barry on 10th April 1989. Restoration in progress.

212 3845 Purchased for the Brighton Works Project and moved from Barry on 9th November 1989. A special ceremony was held at Barry on the day of departure with Dai Woodham and many other people associated with the whole Barry saga present, including the late Robert Adley MP and Capt. Peter Manisty of the ARPS. However, this locomotive was not in fact the last to leave the yard. The engine moved again to the Swindon & Cricklade Railway before going to the Gloucester Warwickshire Railway under ownership of the Dinmore Manor Fund.

213 s 5553 This small prairie was the last to leave Barry, ending a 31 year history of locomotives at Woodham Bros. Purchased privately and moved to a site in Birmingham on 31st January 1990. Then sold to Pete Waterman who had its restoration completed at Tyesley. Interestingly, one of the latest locomotives to steam once more, even though it was the final engine to leave the yard. Currently in use at the West Somerset Railway.

A Standard class 4 and West Country class No. 34101 *Hartland* wait patiently in the lower yard. Both would find new homes in the coming years. *Roger Hardingham*